CONTEMPORARY MARITIME PIRACY IN SOUTHEAST ASIA

IIAS/ISEAS Series on Maritime Issues and Piracy in Asia

Series Advisory Board

The **IIAS/ISEAS Series on Maritime Issues and Piracy in Asia** is an initiative to catalyse research on the topic of piracy and robbery in the Asian seas. Considerable attention in the popular media has been directed to maritime piracy in recent years reflecting the fact/perception that piracy is again a growing concern for coastal nations of the world. The epicentre of global pirate activity is the congested sea-lanes of Southeast Asia but attacks have been registered in wide-scattered regions of the world.

The **International Institute for Asian Studies** (IIAS) is a post-doctoral research centre based in Leiden and Amsterdam, the Netherlands. IIAS' main objective is to encourage Asian studies in the humanities and social sciences — and their interaction with other sciences — by promoting national and international co-operation in these fields. IIAS publications reflect the broad scope of the Institute's interests.

The **Institute of Southeast Asian Studies** (ISEAS) was established in Singapore as an autonomous organization in 1968. It is a regional centre dedicated to the study of socio-political, security and economic trends and developments in Southeast Asia and its wider geostrategic and economic environment. ISEAS Publishing has issued over 2,000 scholarly books and journals since 1972.

IIAS/ISEAS Series on
Maritime Issues and Piracy in Asia

CONTEMPORARY MARITIME PIRACY IN SOUTHEAST ASIA
History, Causes and Remedies

Adam J. Young

IIAS

International Institute for Asian Studies,
The Netherlands

ISEAS

Institute of Southeast Asian Studies,
Singapore

First published in Singapore in 2007 by
ISEAS Publishing
Institute of Southeast Asian Studies
30 Heng Mui Keng Terrace
Pasir Panjang
Singapore 119614

E-mail: publish@iseas.edu.sg
Website: http://bookshop.iseas.edu.sg

First published in Europe in 2007 by
International Institute for Asian Studies
P.O. Box 9515
2300 RA Leiden
The Netherlands

E-mail: iias@let.leidenuniv.nl
Website: http://www.iias.nl

The responsibility for facts and opinions in this publication rests exclusively with the author and his interpretations do not necessarily reflect the views or the policy of the publishers or their supporters.

ISEAS Library Cataloguing-in-Publication Data

Young, Adam J.
  Contemporary maritime piracy in Southeast Asia : history, causes and remedies.
  1.   Pirates—Southeast Asia.
  2.   Sea control—International cooperation.
  I.   Title.
DS526.7 Y69   2007

ISBN 978-981-230-407-0 (hard cover)
ISBN 978-981-230-731-6 (PDF)

Typeset by Superskill Graphics Pte Ltd
Printed in Singapore by Seng Lee Press Pte Ltd

Contents

Acknowledgements

There are of course many people who have lent their time and expertise in helping shape this book. In particular, I would like to thank Mark Valencia who has supported, guided, and most indispensably critiqued this work along the way; Barbara Andaya who guided the early directions and shape of this work, making valuable suggestions and encouraging this project from the start; and Ric Trimillos who helped reign things in with a friendly smile. I would also like to acknowledge the International Institute for Asian Studies at the University of Leiden for providing time, space and the financial wherewithal to edit and refine this project.

On a more personal note, I would like to thank all those friends who lent their shoulders in tough times and celebrated in good. I would also like to acknowledge my family, especially Mom and Dad (Mary and Wayne), Anne Pinkney, and my brother Aaron for their love and support through all times and their encouragement to follow my heart.

All these people are important contributors to this work in their own ways, and deserve a large share of the credit for what is of value and worth in this project, but all analysis, mistakes, and errors are solely the author's responsibility.

Glossary of Selected Terms

Key: AR = Arabic; IN = Indonesian; GR = Greek; L = Latin;
ML = Malay; PH = Philippines

adat (IN/ML)	custom or tradition
anak raja (IN/ML)	child of royalty
animo furandi (L)	legal terminology meaning with the intent to steal, used to connote private motivation for crime as opposed to political motivations
angkatan (IN)	a branch of the armed forces in this context, for example, *angkatan laut*, the armed forces of the sea, i.e., the navy
bajak laut (IN)	pirate
Bajau Laut (Tausug, Sama)	a predominantly seafaring group, part of a larger ethnic group termed the Bajau found through much of southern Philippines, western Malaysia, and parts of northern and eastern Indonesia; self-identified as a separate ethnic group
bangkong	a version of a style of large war boats used in many regions of Borneo and the Malay world into the nineteenth century
berani (IN)	brave, daring
bersenjata (IN)	to be armed

daerah (IN)   a region or area

Darul Islam (IN/AR)   Islamic political movement in Aceh
                                       during the 1950s seeking greater
                                       autonomy within Indonesia; literally
                                       means "abode of Islam", a concept
                                       suggesting the unity of Islam in the
                                       world, as opposed to everything outside
                                       this unity which is in conflict

De Jure Belli ac Pacis (L)   "On the Laws of War and Peace"

gerakan (IN)   a movement

hadapi (IN)   to face or encounter

hostes humani generis (L)   literally means the enemy (*hostes*) of all
                                       mankind (*humani generis*)

ideologi (IN)   ideology

Ilanun (ML)   transliteration of Iranun, an ethnic group
                                       centred on the southern Philippines, and
                                       frequently a general term used to mean
                                       pirate, but usually in specific reference
                                       to the sea raids carried out by the Iranun,
                                       or raids similar in style

jihad (AR)   commonly understood as Islamic holy
                                       war to spread or defend the faith

joanga   a large war boat typically powered by
                                       sail as well as oars, commonly used by
                                       raiders emanating from the southern
                                       Philippines in the eighteenth and
                                       nineteenth centuries

kabupaten (IN)   Administrative unit below a province in
                                       Indonesia

kapal (IN)	A ship, usually a larger metal ship, as opposed to a smaller wooden sailing vessel like the *prahu*
kepemimpinan (IN)	leadership, noun form
Lanun (ML)	see Ilanun
laporan (IN)	a report
laskar (IN)	paramilitary troops
mangayaw (several PH languages)	Diverse practice of sea raiding historically found in much of the Philippines
mare clausum (L)	a sea coming under the control of one nation, as opposed to *mare liberum*, a sea open to the navigation of all nations
melaut (IN)	to go to sea, as opposed to "mendarat" meaning to go landward
menyusul (IN)	to follow, one after another
merdeka (IN)	freedom, independence
Nakhoda (IN/ML)	title of honour usually for a ship's captain or navigator
nasional (IN)	national
nelayan (IN)	fishermen
Orang Kaya (ML)	Malay title literally meaning "rich person"
Orang Laut (IN/ML)	literally "people of the sea" or "sea people"; used in reference with many sea going peoples in the Malay world

parang (IN/ML)   large utility knife or type of machete

peirato (GR)   used in reference to belligerents in the Eastern Mediterranean in the second century BCE; also commonly translated as pirate

pelarian (IN)   literally means "those who run away"; refugee or fugitive

pembaruan (IN)   renewal, reform, or modernization

pembajakan (IN)   piracy, in a generic sense; could be used for software piracy or sea piracy

pirata (L)   used to describe maritime peoples living beyond Roman state control; also commonly translated as pirate

prahu (IN/ML)   small sea-going craft, usually single outboard rigger with sail

republik (IN)   Republic

rompak (pe, pe-an) (IN/ML)   verb form commonly translated as piracy (*perompuk*: pirate, *perompakan*: piracy)

siap (IN)   prepared

suara (IN)   a voice

tak (IN)   colloquial form of *tidak*, meaning no; used to negate a verb or adjective

takut (IN)   to be afraid

Temenggong (ML)   title of honour

tentara (IN)   military armed forces; the army *usir* (IN)   to chase away

Wawasan Nusantara (IN)   literally the Archipelago Concept, a
                                     phrase evoking the notion of the unity
                                     of the Indonesian archipelago

1

Introduction

It was a pertinent and true answer which was made to Alexander the Great by a pirate whom he had seized. When the king asked him what he meant by infesting the sea, the pirate defiantly replied: "The same as you do when you infest the whole world; but because I do it with a little ship I am called a robber, and because you do it with a great fleet, you are an emperor."

— St Augustine[1]

Lord I'm no thief, but a man can go wrong when he's busted.
The food that we canned last summer is gone, and I'm busted.
The fields are all bare and the cotton won't grow,
Me and my family gotta pack up and go.
Where well make a livin the Lord only knows,
And I'm busted.

— Johnny Cash[2]

This book explores the security problematique of contemporary maritime piracy in Southeast Asia, using historical context to highlight causative factors of piracy, and provide insight into why piracy has expanded in scope and frequency over the last fifteen years in the region. This understanding will suggest several remedial approaches in order to address the roots of contemporary maritime piracy in Southeast Asia. These approaches will emphasize the need for building national capacities of states in the region, emphasizing long-term structural development, increased operational policing capabilities, better information gathering, and international co-operation.

Incidents of maritime piracy in Southeast Asia have increased dramatically during the last decade of the twentieth century and into the first years of the new millennium.[3] Piracy, however, has been a persistent presence in the waters of Southeast Asia for approximately 2,000 years up to and including the last fifteen years, evolving with social and political changes in the region over the centuries. The nature of the waters of Southeast Asia,[4] the meeting place of the Pacific and Indian Oceans, an ancient as well as contemporary crossroad, makes them strategically vital, economically and militarily. Contemporarily it is the importance of these waterways that has made piracy an important security issue in Southeast Asia. Seaborne trade accounts for roughly 80 per cent of world trade,[5] approximately one-quarter to one-third of which passes through the Singapore and Malacca Straits and into the Bay of Bengal and the Indian Ocean, or into the South China Sea and the Pacific Ocean beyond. These waters connect the oil fields of the Middle East with the energy-hungry economies of China, Japan and the Koreas, accounting for approximately 80 per cent of Japan's oil.[6] South Korea which has no domestic oil reserves, imports approximately 2.1 million barrels daily, and China imports approximately 5.56 million barrels daily, much of which comes through the Straits of Malacca and Singapore.[7] Moreover, current estimates suggest 150 to 500 ships (large freighters and tankers, not including local traffic) pass through the Strait of Malacca daily,[8] which is upwards of 50,000 ships annually. These waterways are also the shortest route between the Pacific and Indian Ocean theatres of operation for regional and extra-regional navies, such as the United States, Russia, India, China, and Japan. Any threat to the security of these vital sea lanes will be considered seriously.

Beyond posing a direct threat to human life and monetary cost, one of the biggest worries is that a pirate attack against an oil tanker, or other vessel carrying hazardous materials, may cause an accident that even if unintentional could result in an environmental catastrophe, potentially closing off shipping (ironically reducing the number of targets for pirates), and destroying fisheries that provide a livelihood for thousands if not millions of maritime-oriented peoples in the region.[9] Additionally, as Stanley Weeks notes "Piracy raises insurance rates, restricts free trade, increases tensions between the affected littoral states, their neighbours and the countries whose flagged ships are attacked or hijacked."[10] Additionally, there is the potential economic fall out stemming from damage done to regional states' reputations, as shipping companies may choose alternative ports and routes to avoid the threat of piracy.

Adding to the seriousness of these threats is the apparent involvement of organized crime, allegations of state involvement, or at least complicity, in piracy and the conflation of piracy and terrorism.[11] Even though piracy has gained some measure of attention through these connections, it is primarily a low-level security threat in a highly strategic zone and is predominantly endangering local commerce and lives. The resurgence of piracy in the region is symbolic and symptomatic of weak economic and political development that has not kept pace with the rapidly changing economies and societies, and ultimately represents a challenge to the legitimacy of regional states that is not being effectively met.

In a region where maritime security has come into the foreground of regional security concerns,[12] piracy in Southeast Asia is a threat gaining increasing attention as a transnational security issue that demands multilateral and international attention. However, the domestic priority accorded to piracy by the littoral nations of Southeast Asia, combined with fears of internationalizing security in the region and perceived threats to national sovereignty, has hindered effective international and multilateral co-operation. International attention is also predominantly focused on high-end piracy attacks orchestrated by organized criminal networks, particularly as they are conflated with terrorism, ignoring the vast majority of lower-end piracy, which is largely motivated by issues of poverty and disenfranchisement that afflicts vulnerable targets like fishermen and local traders. Thus policies from these forums do not address the motivations of the vast majority of piracy. Additionally, the multilateral and international efforts that are trying to address piracy are focusing on short-term solutions such as co-operative patrols, which are important and useful, but ultimately are like trimming the leaves of a particularly invasive weed rather than pulling it out by its roots.

The roots of contemporary maritime piracy in Southeast Asia lay in the cultural, economic, and political environment of states in the region, and their inability to effectively control or regulate this environment. Various socio-cultural views, economic growth without concomitant political development, poverty and inefficient distribution of wealth, and fragmented or challenged political hegemony, are some of the roots of piracy both historically and contemporarily. These continuities, among others that will be discussed in the coming pages, highlight perennial problems that are structural in nature. Accordingly, policies aimed at addressing piracy need to prioritize structural development such as economic development in coastal regions, dealing with rampant corruption, settling immediate threats to national integrity, and providing various elements of society with a stake in the national economy and identity.

Contemporary maritime piracy in Southeast Asia has been shaped by modern economic, political, and social forces, but it did not evolve in a vacuum. Indeed, maritime piracy has been a reality in Southeast Asia for centuries. There is a continuous thread of piracy that has evolved and adapted over the centuries, trailing from current times to the limits of recorded antiquity in the region, which can provide insight into contemporary phenomena.

WORKING DEFINITION OF PIRACY

There are no essential qualities of piracy; no platonic ideal of piracy hovering in the ether which can be contained in one definition, even in legal terms. There are only approaches to understanding piracy, each with agendas and goals that shape piracy into a convenient form for that particular discussion, very much including this book. The agenda for this book's approach to piracy is to define piracy flexibly and make it applicable to the context of contemporary Southeast Asia, and therefore acceptable for analysis as a security problem. The first section will explore several epistemological issues in discussing piracy, looking at the inherent subjectivity of the term and how this relates to the research presented in this book. Next, in constructing the working definition of piracy, a brief history of the evolution of the Western term "piracy" is presented, as an introduction to how modern international law on piracy evolved. This section will also be used as an introduction to Western concepts of piracy that will be discussed further in Chapter 2 as they interacted with historical concepts of piracy in Southeast Asia. Then two definitions of piracy under international law will be looked at — Article 101 from the United Nations Convention on the Law of the Sea (UNCLOS), and Article 3 from the Convention for the Suppression of Unlawful Acts Against the Safety of Maritime Navigation (SUA) — and the influential International Maritime Bureau's (IMB) definition that is very common in the media and security literature, but is not a legally binding definition. The UNCLOS and SUA definitions will also be further discussed in Chapter 3, starting on p. 80, in terms of their policy implications, and issues surrounding the IMB definition will be discussed further in Chapter 4 starting on p. 122. Drawing on these definitions, a working definition of piracy for this book will be presented and discussed.

Epistemological Considerations

The study of piracy is fraught with epistemological problems, for as with "the word 'crime' itself ... 'piracy' is a term that both describes and passes a (negative) judgment ... addresses an object that is *a priori* normatively defined, and is based primarily on sources in which this value judgment goes without saying."[13] Although the literature used for this book by and large is grounded in a negative assessment of piracy, there have been several notable attempts to portray piracy without moralizing, and yet trying not to minimize its brutal reality.[14] An objective stance is important because the topic of maritime piracy in Southeast Asia is approached using a vocabulary rooted in a particular Western academic, cultural paradigm far removed from the reality of historical and contemporary piracy.

Post-modern critiques, and the whole debate surrounding Orientalism initiated by the late Edward Said, make us more aware of using outside definitions to describe local phenomenon such as piracy in Southeast Asia. As Said suggests, however, while it is impossible to divorce oneself from one's intellectual heritage totally, the effort can be made to free one's research from biases, and in the case of piracy a self-conscious awareness of indigenous perspectives can help alleviate this situation.[15] This goal is complicated, however, by the ubiquitous complaint and fact that indigenous sources are scarce in Southeast Asia, both historically and contemporarily. Accounts of Southeast Asian piracy largely derive from foreign sources: Chinese, Arabic, and later, European. In this situation judicious use of foreign accounts and ethnographic studies is quite helpful, but still problematic for trying to understand piracy in Southeast Asia, and this will be addressed in Chapter 2. As we move into the modern era there is plenty of literature on piracy, but there is still a general lack of local Southeast Asian scholarship on contemporary piracy.

A major limitation of the approaches to contemporary piracy used in this book is that they address piracy on macro-level scales, making generalizations across maritime Southeast Asia. While these generalizations are useful in establishing broad approaches to addressing piracy, and effectively highlight perennial issues contributing to cycles of piracy, they lack local details that could provide an important depth to the discussion. From historical accounts there is material available on this local scale, and much of it has been incorporated into the historical discussions of this book. However, this kind of material is not available for contemporary piracy, so comparison and contrast on this scale is difficult. When possible, generalizations are avoided, and it is in part to this end that a diverse spectrum of historic case studies were chosen. However, where these generalizations directly impact on analysis and discussion they are specifically noted. In discussions of contemporary piracy there is almost no attempt to avoid generalizations across cultures, because there is no research that the author is aware of on which to base analysis of different peoples and different practices of piracy. In fact there is very little primary research on contemporary piracy and so generalizations for the time being must be accepted, with the tacit recognition that they are being made. The limitations of the approaches to piracy used for this book should be taken as important future directions of research and analysis of piracy in Southeast Asia, addressing the "local" and focusing more closely on the people themselves, both impacted by and engaging in these activities.

In this book, piracy is always understood as a subjective concept as it is problematic in definition and has been subject to a multitude of different understandings over centuries of use. However, for the sake of practicality the word "piracy" will only appear in quotes when its subjective nature requires particular attention, or of course when in a direct quote. In order to clarify the terminology that will be used in the following discussions of piracy, the word "piracy" will be used mainly to refer to those predatory maritime activities that are carried out by agents *without* the acknowledged support of a recognized, legitimate political entity. While still vague, it offers a contrast to "raiding" (in a Southeast Asian context) or "privateering" (in a Western context), which will be used to refer to those predatory maritime activities that *had* the support or acknowledgement of a recognized legitimate political entity. This delineation between piracy and raiding/privateering involves a large grey area as there could be a fluid movement of agents between legitimacy and illegitimacy, but overall it provides a useful framework for future discussions. These terms will also frequently be interchanged according to the perspective from which they are viewed. For example, Spanish views of Iranun predatory activities were frequently referred to as "piracy", but the Iranun perspective saw it as "raiding". In this respect when multiple view points are being addressed "piracy/raiding" may be used to show this ambiguity of perspective. In discussions of the contemporary period this becomes less problematic as distinctions between illegitimate and legitimate piracy largely disappear.

Western Definitions

Modern international law on piracy evolved largely from Western legal history, shaped in part by the expansion of European economic interests and political power into Southeast Asia. The concept of piracy in a Western tradition has evolved and developed over at least 2,000 years, being reinterpreted to fit the needs of the times. The word itself originated from Greek and Latin, the words *peirato* and *pirata* both connoting political legitimacy or belligerency; the former being those *included* under the Roman hegemony, and the latter being those who lived a way of life *outside* Roman hegemony, and therefore illegitimate.[16] Certain concepts in the law of piracy became particularly important, such as criminality,[17] *animo furandi*,[18] and *hostes humani generis*,[19] which evolved from medieval and renaissance interpretations of ancient classical literature, where the word *pirata* changed in meaning from a belligerent in the context of war, to mean an unauthorized privateer. It described a risk of participating in the burgeoning trade of the times, but it was not yet considered in terms of criminality.[20]

In the sixteenth and seventeenth centuries influential publicists and jurists such as the Dutchman Hugo Grotius (1583–1645), who is often termed the "father of modern international law", and the Britisher John Selden (1584–1654) were redefining the concept of piracy, based in large part on the need to defend expanding trade networks throughout the world, and particularly in maritime Southeast Asia. Grotius conceived of piracy as a criminal disturbance of lawful commerce, thereby in conflict with states' sovereignty. Therefore, state jurisdiction could be extended through naval occupation of waters, just as in the military occupation of land, thus providing impetus for justifying martial action to protect commerce.[21] Selden's classic *Mare Clausum* was directed at extending a particular interpretation of maritime law that would allow England to claim parts of the seas in a quasi-occupation,[22] and thus also extend their municipal jurisdiction on the seas. These interpretations justified using military navies in defense of trade, as policemen, without having to declare war and thus abide by the rules of war. Moreover, this interpretation coincided with imperialist needs to deal with Southeast Asian "piracy".

Complicating European practice and understandings of piracy as a criminal activity was the wide use of privateers. Privateers in international law were defined as "vessels belonging to private owners, and sailing under commission of war empowering the person to whom it is granted to carry on all forms of hostility which are permissible at sea by the usages of war."[23] The use of privateers to supplement meagre naval forces in time of war was a standard practice among Western states from the thirteenth to the nineteenth century. Privateers were a resource of skilled mariners that the state did not have to pay for, and could actually provide revenue. Empowering non-state actors with legitimatized means of violence, however, had its dangers, as reining in privateers once their purpose had been served often proved difficult. As a result of frequent wars in Europe, combined with the practice of privateering, piracy became rampant by the seventeenth and early eighteenth centuries in European "controlled" waters,[24] as Daniel Defoe noted in the beginning of the eighteenth century: "Privateers in time of war are a nursery for Pyrates against a Peace."[25] In the nineteenth century, by the time Britain had become *the* naval power in the world,[26] privateering, which had become a weapon of the weak (those nations that couldn't afford a large standing navy), was finally outlawed by the majority of European naval powers in the Declaration of Paris in 1858 (at Britain's behest), following the end of the Crimean War.[27] The nineteenth century was the official end of "legitimate piracy" in the West and these attitudes would be brought to bear on local practices of piracy in Southeast Asia, as well as forming the underpinnings of modern international law on piracy.

United Nations Convention on the Law of the Sea

The Western evolution of the concept of piracy, in part stimulated by economic and political circumstances arising in Southeast Asia, led directly to the definition of piracy incorporated in the 1958 Geneva Conventions, the United Nations Convention on the Law of the Sea (UNCLOS I), the 1960 UNLCOS II negotiations, and finally the 1982 United Nations Convention of the Law of the Sea (UNCLOS III) that was put into force.[28] Article 101 of UNCLOS defines piracy as follows:

> *Article 101*
> *Definition of "piracy"*
> "piracy" consists of any of the following acts:
> (a) any illegal acts of violence or detention, or any act of depredation, committed for private ends by the crew or the passengers of a private ship or a private aircraft, and directed:
> > (i) on the high seas, against another ship or aircraft, or against persons or property on board such ship or aircraft;
> > (ii) against a ship, aircraft, persons or property in a place outside the jurisdiction of any State;
> (b) any act of voluntary participation in the operation of a ship or of an aircraft with knowledge of facts making it a pirate ship or aircraft;

(c) any act of inciting or of intentionally facilitating an act described in subparagraph (a) or (b).[29]

Of particular concern in Southeast Asia is the requirement that piracy takes place beyond the jurisdiction of any state, on the high seas, as piracy frequently occurs in territorial waters, excluding piracy in strategic choke points like the Singapore and Malacca Straits. Another concern is that under UNCLOS piracy requires ship-to-ship conflict, which could exclude crimes in port. Additionally, the exclusion of political acts is seen as problematic for many, although this book's working definition supports this. These issues will also be discussed in more detail in Chapter 3 starting on p. 80.[30]

Convention for the Suppression of Unlawful Acts Against the Safety of Maritime Navigation

SUA was not designed to address definitional or jurisdictional issues of piracy *per se*, but rather was meant to address international terrorism,[31] although it is being promulgated as an anti-piracy document,[32] partially in order to address some of the perceived deficiencies in UNCLOS noted above. Article 3 of SUA outlines a broad definitional framework of acts that constitute a threat to maritime navigation. It sidesteps definitional pitfalls by not mentioning any specific acts such as "piracy" or "terrorism", but rather referring to

1. Any person who commits an offence if that person unlawfully or intentionally:
   a. seizes or exercises control over a ship by force or threat thereof or any other form of intimidation; or
   b. performs an act of violence against a person onboard a ship if that act is likely to endanger the safe navigation of that ship[33]

Despite its ability to sidestep some of the problems inherent in UNCLOS, SUA also raises many issues, including concerns of national sovereignty, its utility in addressing piracy given the vague terms it would use to describe piracy, and the fact that it was designed as an anti-terrorism convention. These issues have caused reluctance on the part of key maritime nations in Southeast Asia to accede to the Convention. As with UNCLOS, these issues will be addressed in more detail in Chapter 3 starting on p. 80. Also see Appendix A for further details on SUA.

The International Maritime Bureau

The International Maritime Bureau (IMB) is a subsection of the International Chamber of Commerce's Commercial Crime Services (ICC Commercial Crime Services, abbreviated as ICC), a private organization whose task is "to prevent fraud in international trade and maritime transport, reduce the risk of piracy and assist law enforcement in protecting crews".[34] Further in this chain is the Piracy Reporting Centre (PRC), a division of the ICC-IMB, started in 1992 in Kuala Lumpur, Malaysia, which focuses on piracy.[35] The IMB Piracy Reporting Centre (IMB-PRC) is a key hub for disseminating piracy information such as statistics and area warnings where recent hotspots of pirate activity have been reported. The IMB-PRC statistics have become ubiquitous in literature and media dealing with piracy. The statistics coming out of the IMB are a driving force in discussions of piracy, from policy literature to mass media, and deserve special attention. Issues surrounding the ubiquity of IMB statistics will be further addressed in Chapter 4.

The IMB defines piracy as: "An act of boarding or attempting to board any ship with the intent to commit theft or any other crime and with the intent or capability to use force in the furtherance of that act."[36] Interestingly the definition that the IMB uses for collecting their information is not legally binding, and does not conform to international legal definitions like Article 101 from UNCLOS, Article 3 from SUA, or the national laws of any country. As a non-binding definition used for their collection of statistics the IMB is at liberty to disregard jurisdictional concerns as well as nuances of definition such as *animo furandi* versus political motivations.

Working Definition of Piracy

- **Working definition of piracy**: An act of boarding or attempting to board any ship with the intent to commit theft or any other crime and with the intent or capability to use force in the furtherance of that act, excepting those crimes that are shown or strongly suspected to be politically motivated.

The working definition of piracy for this book essentially follows the IMB definition of piracy, but purposefully separates out politically motivated maritime crime. This definition is being used for similar reasons why the IMB uses it — to more accurately reflect the dangers faced by the victims;[37] an inclusive understanding that ignores what has become a hallmark of the modern piracy problematique — jurisdiction. Jurisdiction is an important consideration in how best to tailor policy to address piracy, and will be discussed at some length in Chapter 3. It often complicates assessing what the real issues behind piracy are that need to be addressed. The UNCLOS definition would exclude the majority of incidents of piracy in Southeast Asia as they occur in the territorial waters of states. This working definition draws in for analysis a plethora of maritime criminal activity under the rubric of piracy, which will in turn allow a gross dissection of the phenomena to facilitate figuring out why it has become a problem once again, and how it can best be dealt with.

Politically motivated crime was left out of this definition, unlike the IMB and SUA definitions of piracy, because rather than helping to clarify the issue of piracy it clouds it in jurisdictional issues of national sovereignty and associated international power struggles. Moreover, the conflation of piracy and terrorism itself is questionable as there are important philosophical differences in the maritime violence perpetrated by each. Terrorists are motivated by broader political goals and want to draw attention to themselves, which to a pirate could endanger the furtherance of their primary motive, personal gain. For example, the worst case scenario of an oil tanker or other large vessel being scuttled in the straits as part of a terrorist plot could be detrimental to the livelihoods of pirates, as trade would likely be shut down for an indefinite period of time. Additionally, while terrorism is frequently linked to religious motivations, there is no evidence of religiously motivated piracy for private gain, i.e. specific targets are not chosen based on religion.

Terrorism has often been conflated with piracy as there are tempting potential operational links and potential overlap in tactics and goals at the high end of piracy when vessels are hijacked.[38] However, perceived links and potential connections have been played down in recent months following the Tri-annual Conference on Piracy and Maritime Terrorism, held in Kuala Lumpur in June 2004, sponsored by the International Maritime Bureau. Senior Advisor for Rand Corporation, Brian Jenkins, a recognized expert on terrorism, announced the general conclusion of the conference that "I don't think it is appropriate to blend the increasing problem of piracy with the potentially more dangerous consequences of terrorism ..."[39] Captain P. K. Mukundan, director of the ICC-IMB, reiterated this, saying that there was "nothing to show that terrorists and pirates have joined up".[40] At the closing round table discussion of The Workshop on Maritime Security, Maritime Terrorism and Piracy in Asia, held in Singapore in September 2004, similar conclusions were also drawn. These important distinctions and separations between piracy and terrorism indicate that different approaches need to be taken in addressing the root causes of each, although in controlling the symptoms there will be some potential overlap as increased operational capacities may affect both pirates and potential maritime terrorists.[41]

TYPOLOGY OF CONTEMPORARY MARITIME PIRACY IN SOUTHEAST ASIA

This typology describes phenomena based on the working definition of piracy detailed above, placed on a fluid scale that "corresponds to an escalating scale of risk and return. As the risk and potential return increase so do the threat and degree of violence ... [and] so does the apparent degree of organization of the attackers."[42] See Figure 1.1. This typology of piracy should not be seen as a concrete construction, because in the real world there is likely to be a fluid movement of agents depending on specific circumstances between various points on this

FIGURE 1.1

Typology of Piracy

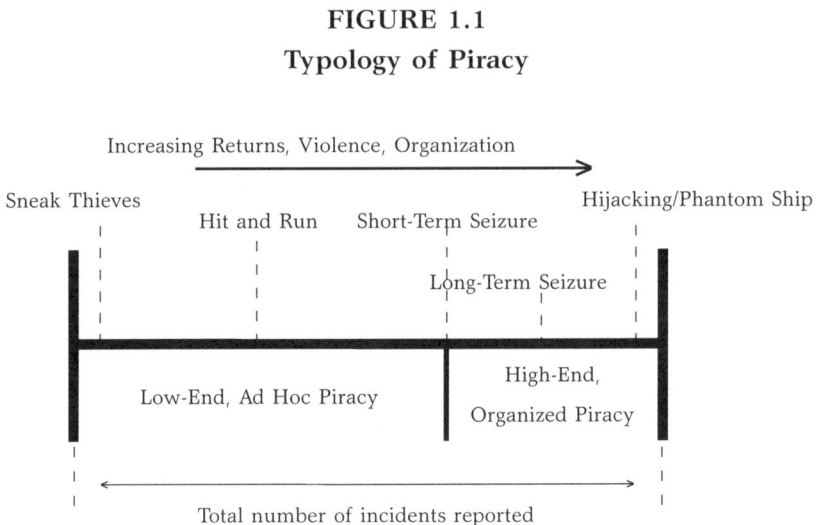

Note: Hypothetical representation of typology of piracy as a proportion of total incidents, with placement of various kinds of piracy on the scale.

scale, and there is no absolute rules separating the use of violence, expected returns and organization. Along this line, the typology is not predictive of behavior, but rather descriptive of recorded incidents. On one side of the scale is low-end ad hoc piracy with relatively less chance of violence, lower expected returns and less risk, and on the other side is high-end organized piracy with relatively higher expected returns, a greater chance of violence, and requires more organization and risks on the part of the pirates. Contemporarily there are many levels of piracy active in maritime Southeast Asia; "the criminals run the gamut from the maritime equivalent of bank robbers ... to members of well-connected and well-organized rings that can arrange for transfers of large quantities of stolen cargo at sea or at port without detection."[43] Piracy includes everything from petty theft to the hijacking of entire vessels, and pirates could be anyone from opportunistic fishermen, to members of syndicates and even rogue military units.[44]

The most common incidents of piracy are on the low end of the typology and can be classified as sea-robbery, simple hit-and-run thefts involving individuals to small gangs with ad hoc organization, which usually result in violence only if confronted.[45] Within this category, attacks against fishermen and other local traffic make up the probable majority of incidents. The next level involves the short-term seizure of a vessel, often for less than 30 minutes, but the crew is held hostage and often threatened or inflicted with violence to reveal locations of valuables, such as the vessel's safe. This step up requires more people, more equipment and, therefore, more organization, and can also involve more violence and greater returns for their efforts, although the attacks still appear to be largely opportunistic. These seizures often end up on the low end of the typology, but can also move towards the high-end spectrum as all the variables involved can move towards the high end of the scale. An example of this is the attack on the *Valiant Carrier,* a fuel oil tanker that was forcibly stopped with Molotov cocktails, where the crew was threatened and in two cases received injuries.[46] The twelve attackers made off with the ship's electronics and other valuables, but were not interested in the cargo. These attacks are also serious because, as was the case with the *Valiant Carrier,* the ships are left uncontrolled for much of the attack, creating a serious risk of collision and the potential for an environmental disaster.

At the top of the scale on the high-end organized side are long-term and permanent seizures where the entire ship is ransacked, or the target was the cargo itself, often valuable and/or easily resellable goods such as palm oil, fuel oil, electronics, or refined metal ores. The ships themselves can also become a target. These ships are called "phantom ships" because they simply disappear; the ships are repainted and reflagged (registering the ship with a different nation). Often the ship's name can be changed multiple times, as these services are provided via the Internet. Like stolen cars on land, these ships are often used for further illegal activities, such as smuggling goods or scamming cargo shippers by offering cheap shipping costs and then absconding with the cargo.[47] These attacks require greater organization and materials as the entire cargo needs to be dealt with, and necessitate violence as the crew is either subdued for long periods of time or disposed of.[48]

Off the scale as a type of piracy, but interesting to consider, is "social piracy", a concept largely based on Hobsbawm's description of "social banditry", outlined in his book *Bandits*.[49] These pirates rob and attack people outside their own community for the benefit of not only themselves and their families, but their community as well. This type of piracy seems to fall into the low-end scale of piracy, but not necessarily so. This phenomenon will be further examined in Chapter 3 under the section heading "Social Piracy" (p. 65) in a broader context of economic and social marginalization.

APPROACHES TO PIRACY

Policy–History Nexus

Much good research has been directed at examining contemporary maritime piracy in Southeast Asia within certain academic and policy analyst circles, such as those that study maritime security, non-traditional security threats including transnational crime, and "grey area phenomenon" (GAP).[50] This research has provided many useful insights into the nature of contemporary piracy in Southeast Asia, and is at the heart of a growing effort to combat this resurgent phenomenon. The academic discipline of history has also provided many good accounts describing and contextualizing past practices of piracy, to which this book is much indebted. However, each of these disciplines dealing with maritime piracy is mutually unconscious or largely unconcerned with each other's material.

Most policy literature dealing with piracy seems to assume the supremacy of the present, the unfolding of contemporary affairs in "real time" "realpolitik", to which history is simply the past, what came before the important events of today. Continuities and/or change are assumed rather than examined or analysed. Accordingly, historical context is often lacking or treated simplistically, largely outside the scope of their discussion. This leads to broad assumptions that surreptitiously link phenomenon over vast stretches of time or ignore important threads of continuity. Moreover, this process leads toward a lack of contextualization within the socio-political and cultural framework of Southeast Asia, the biggest hotspot of contemporary piracy in the world. While much policy literature has focused on the present, historical accounts of piracy are frequently isolated from contemporary circumstances, making them quite literally "academic" in their usefulness to analysts.[51] However, in order to better understand the roots of contemporary piracy in Southeast Asia, the context from which it has emerged, including the historical context of piracy and its links to modern piracy, need to be explored.

Piracy is not a new phenomenon in the waters of Southeast Asia, so in order to better understand it we must look to the past for what it can tell us. This use of history is not to advocate the cliché that those who do not learn from history are doomed to repeat it because this book recognizes that contemporary phenomenon are in many ways distinct from their antecedents. They are phenomena largely shaped by a modern world, but a modern world and phenomena that did not spring from a void, or from a clean slate. As Michael Aung-Thwin has purported for Burmese history, and as a possible model for understanding Southeast Asian history broadly, "strength was maintained and expressed by spirals or structural cycles, a process of expansion and contraction of the same institutions, rather than the elimination of old ones, and the creation of fundamentally new ones."[52] In this situation the continuity of history is assumed and change must be proven. The nature of this book precludes any kind of detailed examination of such an assertion with respect to piracy, but it is a pertinent reminder for those dealing with contemporary Southeast Asia to give due regard to the past.

There are some notable works in recent years that have moved in the direction of utilizing both history and policy literature,[53] but the majority of academic and policy literature on piracy still seems largely uninformed about the other, or simply outside their professional concern. This book seeks to contribute to bridging the gap between historical context and policy analysis of piracy, and from this broader understanding suggest ways and means of addressing the root causes of contemporary maritime piracy in Southeast Asia.

State Approaches to Piracy

The state is the focal point of analysis for this book. It is primarily a discussion of a contemporary security threat from a criminal enterprise, and as such revolves around what is being threatened: lives, the environment, trade, and fundamentally the threat posed by piracy and what its existence symbolizes, to the integrity and legitimacy of affected states. Piracy could be analysed from numerous perspectives, such as through processes of globalization, as it is an important factor affecting the economic and political context from which maritime piracy has re-emerged. However, piracy in Southeast Asia is not a security threat to processes of globalization, but to the state. Moreover, piracy in Southeast Asia does not emerge from globalization but from within the territory of particular states. The state, and relations between the international system of states, is the central feature of contemporary policy.

The state is also an important link to the history of piracy as much historical analysis has focused on the emergence of "states" and authority structures in the region. Understanding how piracy fit into these structures, framing the perceived legitimacy and illegitimacy of piracy, and how these perceptions change through time and across cultures, is an important factor in understanding how historical context is relevant in addressing contemporary maritime piracy. In the past, as today, the tenuous control exerted by state structures was often disregarded by non-state agents, as they often acted independently of state power until they could be brought back under control again.[54]

Two primary understandings of states and their authority will be used. First, in discussion of historic power structures in Southeast Asia, and in analysing cultural continuities, a flexible state structure based on an understanding of authority rooted in concepts of charismatic leadership will be predominantly used. For discussion of European, colonial, and modern nation-states, a state model based on Weberian understandings of power will be emphasized. In this model, power is based on the monopolistic control of violence within proscribed territorial boundaries. Underlying both these aspects of the state is a current of neo-liberal capitalist thought that emphasizes the role of economic processes in the exercise of state power.

An intriguing aspect of piracy is the state's role in defining understandings of piracy, both historically and contemporarily. However, in both systems these lines were frequently blurred, and state structures often actively encouraged and supported non-state agents of violence, like privateers, when their activities were to the benefit of the political centre.[55] State control as it regards piracy is a dynamic system of power and depends on who has the authority to determine political legitimacy and illegitimacy through agreement or assent of its people, or by force and persuasion.[56]

States have provided structure and organization for piracy both in terms of support and resistance. When states have directly supported piracy they have lent it the official authority and structure of the state itself, but when states have actively suppressed piracy they have also given it structure, defining it as opposite of the state, in contrast to its goals. Until the nineteenth century the boundary between state support and state suppression was frequently blurred, and continues to this day to present problems due to implications of state complicity. Because the frame of reference for piracy has been so thoroughly incorporated with states, either in co-operation or in contrast, the measure of piracy is to what extent a given state can exert its control. Does the state have sufficient control to disperse any non-state condoned maritime activity? In any given arena through time and space where a state claims some kind of authority, does it have the power or desire to control non-state actors, or even those within the state structure, and what are the implications for piracy? Does the state have the capacity or will to control the economic, social, and political processes stimulating piracy? Does or can the state control the physical means of enacting piracy?

To address these questions and issues, three aspects of state control that extend across historical and contemporary piracy will be focused on. First, the state's ability to exert some minimal control over the people in its territory through "binding commands, rules, and laws backed by force" and reciprocal social contracts, thereby controlling those who become the agents of piracy.[57] Second, the state's ability to maintain a political hegemony by dominating and controlling the use of violence, as piracy is an eruption of unauthorized violence through gaps in state control. Piracy is an illegitimate hub of power, which itself further widens these gaps and questions the state's ability to control, and/or regulate, the means of its own legitimacy in the eyes of its people and the international community. Third, the state's ability to control the tools, intelligence, and tactics of piracy as it impacts pirate's success vis-à-vis the state, because of the direct connection to the capabilities of pirates. Moreover, they have been a primary focus of contemporary policy addressing piracy, and thus necessary of discussion. Overall, the weaker state control in these areas the more piracy flourishes, and the further compromised the state's ability to regain control. The relative success of the state in carrying out these projects is at the heart of piracy.

All of these aspects of state control will be discussed within the context of Southeast Asia, with particular focus on the largest archipelagic state in the world, Indonesia, which consistently accounts for half or more piracy incidents in Southeast Asia, and more than one-quarter of incidents in the world. Indonesia is widely perceived as a weak link in maritime security of the region in part because of the impact of the Asian economic crisis of the late 1990s, and the resulting political turmoil.

ORGANIZATION OF CHAPTERS

Chapter 1 has presented a description of the goals of this book, the nature of the problem to be examined, the approach that will be used, some consideration of inherent epistemological issues of research, analysis and argument, and a working definition of piracy. Chapter 2 will look at definitions of piracy historically in Southeast Asia, discussing the applicability of the term "piracy" to the context of Southeast Asia. These definitions will then be put in specific contexts of several case studies of historical piracy, highlighting causative factors underlying the development of piracy in the region. This will lay the groundwork for drawing and analysing continuities between causative factors past and present, which will suggest ways of approaching piracy contemporarily. Furthermore, Chapter 2 will discuss the interaction between the historical conceptions of piracy in Southeast Asia with European economic and political expansion in the region, highlighting issues faced by the European powers in suppressing local piracy, which will also provide material for further comparison with the contemporary piracy problematique.

Chapter 3 moves to the contemporary period. Each section deals with causative factors of piracy stemming from issues of state control that contribute to an environment making piracy more thinkable and practicable. The first section will focus on constructing what is motivating piracy, creating a large potential labour pool of piracy that is beyond state control. This discussion will emphasize economic and social marginalization as well as cultural continuities with the socio-cultural matrix of the past. The second section focuses on the state's inability to control the means of its own legitimacy, how piracy has emerged from gaps in this control, and what has caused these gaps to appear. The third section discusses more technical and "practical" reasons why piracy has re-emerged beyond state control, looking at the available tools, intelligence, and tactics of pirates and their ability to create a suite of technology complimentary to the weaknesses of their targets and the state. Chapter 4 will draw on previous discussion presenting several remedial approaches, emphasizing international co-operation, policing, structural development, and information gathering, as a way forward in addressing the roots/causative factors of contemporary maritime piracy in Southeast Asia. The final section will provide brief conclusions, and address the feasibility of these policy directions and what the implications of this are.

Notes

1. Saint Augustine Bishop of Hippo, *The City of God Against the Pagans*, translated and edited by R. W. Dyson (Cambridge: Cambridge University Press, 1998), Bk. IV, ch. 4, 148.
2. Johnny Cash, *Busted*, Columbia Country Records compact disk C3K 65557, CK 65559, DIDP 095201.
3. In the early 1990s piracy began to increase not only in maritime Southeast Asia but all over the world, in parts of the Americas (Brazil, Ecuador, Dominican Republic, Columbia), Africa (Nigeria, Somalia, Angola, Guinea), and the Bay of Bengal (India, Bangladesh, Sri Lanka). Although a worldwide phenomenon, each year for the last twelve years Southeast Asia has accounted for more incidents than any other region in the world ("Piracy and Armed Robbery Against Ships Annual Report", 1 January – 31 December 2003, *Piracy Reporting Centre* [Kuala Lumpur: ICC International Maritime Bureau, 2003], p. 5; "Piracy and Armed Robbery Against Ships Annual Report", 1 January – 31 December 2004, *Piracy Reporting Centre* [Kuala Lumpur: ICC International Maritime Bureau, 2004], p. 5).

    Prior to the International Maritime Bureau (IMB) forming the Piracy Reporting Centre in Kuala Lumpur, which began collecting piracy statistics in 1992, there were hardly any reported incidents of piracy. However, an all time high of 469 incidents were recorded for 2000, and the second highest of 445 incidents were recorded in 2003 ("Piracy Annual Report", 2003, p. 5). Between 1992 and 1999 the average number of incidents reported worldwide was 183, and between 2000 and 2004 the average number of incidents reported worldwide has jumped to 389. Since 1992 Southeast Asia has accounted for approximately 52 per cent of the world total, and Indonesia itself has accounted for 51 per cent of the total incidents in Southeast Asia and 27 per cent of the world total (these averages and percentages were calculated by the author based on statistics provided in the aforementioned Annual Reports). See also Appendix B for

further statistical breakdown of Southeast Asian and Indonesian incidents
of piracy calculated from IMB statistics.

4. The waters of Southeast Asia are taken to *include* the following regions all
    listed as individual regions for which the IMB collects data: the littoral
    states of Southeast Asia, China/Hong Kong/Macau region, Hainan/Luzon/
    Hong Kong Triangle, the Singapore Strait, and the South China Sea, thus
    excluding the contiguous regions of the East China Sea, Northeast Asia, and
    the Bay of Bengal region. These areas will form the regional scope of
    "Southeast Asia" for the rest of this text.

5. Donna J. Nincic, "Sea Lane Security and U.S. Maritime Trade: Choke Points
    as Scarce Resources", in *Globalization and Maritime Power*, edited by Sam J.
    Tangredi (Washington, D.C.: National Defense University Press, 2002),
    p. 145.

6. Donald Urquhart, "Malacca Strait users urged to help pay for safety aids",
    Business Times (Singapore), 14 October 2003, sec. Shipping Times.

7. Country Analysis Briefs, http://www.eia.doe.gov/emeu/cabs/choke.html
    (accessed 9 March 2005).

8. Peter Chalk, *Low Intensity Conflict in Southeast Asia*, Conflict Studies, no.
    305/306 (Warwickshire, England: Research Institute for the Study of Conflict
    and Terrorism, 1998), p. 6.

9. See Sam Vaknin, "Treasure Island Revisited", *Financial News*, 19 July 2002,
    p. 2, from *LexisNexis Academic* online database; Keith Bradsher, "Attacks on
    Chemical Ships in Southeast Asia Seem to be Piracy, Not Terrorism", *New
    York Times*, 27 March 2003, sec. A; Stanley Weeks, "Piracy and Regional
    Security", in *Combating Piracy and Ship Robbery*, edited by Hamzah Ahmad
    and Akira Ogawa (Tokyo: Okazaki Institute, 2001), p. 100; Jason Abbot, and
    Neil Renwick, "Pirates? Maritime Piracy and Societal Security in Southeast
    Asia", *Pacifica Review* 11, no. 1 (February 1999), p. 15; and Peter Chalk,
    "Contemporary Maritime Piracy in Southeast Asia", *Studies in Conflict and
    Terrorism* 21 (March 1997): 91, among many others.

10. Weeks, "Piracy and Regional Security", p. 100.

11. Chalk, *Low Intensity Conflict*, pp. 2–8; Jon Vagg, "Rough Seas?", *British
    Journal of Criminology* 35, no. 1 (1995): 68; Carolin Liss, "Maritime Piracy in
    Southeast Asia", *Southeast Asian Affairs 2003* (Singapore: Institute of Southeast
    Asian Studies, 2003), pp. 54, 62–65.

12. Mark J. Valencia, "Troubled Waters", *Harvard International Review* 16, no. 2
    (Spring 1994): p. 1 of 12, *Academic Search Premier* online database; Mark J.
    Valencia, "Regional Maritime Regime Building: Prospects in Northeast and
    Southeast Asia", *Ocean Development & International Law* 31, no. 3 (Jul–Sep
    2000): 223, p. 1 of 24, *Academic Search Premier* online database; also see
    among others Jin-Hyun Paik, and Anthony Bergin, "Maritime Security in
    the Asia Pacific", in *Asia's Emerging Regional Order*, edited by William T.
    Tow, Ramesh Chandra Thakur, and In-Taek Hyun (Tokyo and New York:
    United Nations University Press, 2000), p. 177.

13. Joseph N.F.M. a Campo, "Discourse without Discussion: Representations of Piracy in Colonial Indonesia 1816–25", *Journal of Southeast Asian Studies* 34, no. 2 (June 2003): 200.

14. In particular see the works of James Warren on Sulu, the Iranun and the Balangingi, the thoughtful article by N.F.M. a Campo on the discourse of piracy, the works of history by Barbara and Leonard Andaya, Dian Murray's work on piracy in southern China, Rubin's work on the law of piracy, and Janice Thomson's look at piracy in European state formation, among others cited in this text.

15. Edward Said, *Orientalism* (New York: Vintage Books, 1978), p. 10.

16. Alfred P. Rubin, *The Law of Piracy*, 2nd ed. (New York: Transnational Publishers, Inc., 1998), p. 10.

17. Criminal in this sense defines actions punishable under local, or municipal, or civil law, as opposed to necessitating recourse to international law or law governing war.

18. Meaning private motives, as opposed to political motives.

19. This phrase literally means "enemy of humankind", or "enemy to all humankind".

20. Rubin, *Law of Piracy*, p. 20.

21. Ibid., p. 41, from Grotius, *De Jure Belli ac Pacis* [On the Laws of War and Peace], Book II, ch. iii, para. 13(2).

22. Monica Brito Vieira, "Mare Liberum vs. Mare Clausum", *Journal of the History of Ideas* 64, no. 3 (July 2003): 371.

23. William Edward Hall, *A Treatise on International Law*, 8th ed., edited by A. Pearce Higgins (Oxford: Clarendon Press, 1924), pp. 620–21, in Janice E. Thomson, *Mercenaries, Pirates, and Sovereigns* (Princeton: Princeton University Press, 1994), p. 22.

24. Philip Gosse, *The History of Piracy* (New York: Tudor Publishing Company, 1934), p. 58.

25. Daniel Defoe, *A General History of the Robberies and Murders of the Most Notorious Pyrates* (New York: Garland Publishing, 1972), Preface, p. A3.

26. This was made possible by a pivotal moment in history when the English Navy in 1805 under the command of Vice Admiral Horatio Lord Nelson (at cost to his own life) defeated the French navy outside the Spanish port of Cadiz, off Cape Trafalgar. See Kenneth J. Hagan, *This People's Navy* (New York: The Free Press, 1991), p. 63.

27. Anne Perotin-Dumon, "The Pirate and the Emperor", in *The Political Economy of Merchant Empires*, edited by James D. Tracy (Cambridge: Cambridge University Press, 1991), p. 222.

28. Unless otherwise specified, UNLCOS from here on will be used to refer to the 1982 UNCLOS III.

29. *United Nations Convention of the Law of the Sea* (Montego Bay, Jamaica, 10 December 1982), Article 101, http://www.un.org/Depts/los/convention_agreements/texts/unclos/closindx.htm (accessed 27 March 2004).

30. See also Appendix A for more information on UNCLOS, including clarification of territorial designations such as "territorial waters".

31. Jay L. Batongbacal, "Trends in Anti-Piracy Cooperation in the ASEAN Region", in *Combating Piracy and Ship Robbery*, edited by Ahmad and Ogawa, p. 125.

32. See, for example, arguments by G. Gerard Ong, "Ships Can Be Dangerous Too", unpublished paper presented at the conference People and the Sea II: Conflicts, Threats and Opportunities, Amsterdam, 1 August 2003, p. 8; Zou Keyuan, "Quelling Sea Piracy in East Asia", unpublished paper presented at the conference People and the Sea II, pp. 4, 8–10; Weeks, "Piracy and Regional Security", p. 101.

33. "Convention for the Suppression of Unlawful Acts Against the Safety of Maritime Navigation" (Rome, 10 March 1988), Article 3, http://edoc.mpil.de/conference-on-terrorism/related/uc.cfm (accessed 27 March 2004).

34. "International Crime Services International Maritime Bureau", http://www.iccwbo.org/ccs/menu_imb_bureau.asp (accessed 27 March 2004).

35. "IMB Piracy Reporting Centre", http://www.icc-ccs.org/prc/overview.php.

36. "Piracy Annual Report", 2003, p. 3.

37. Jayant Abhyankar, "Piracy and Ship Robbery: A Growing Menace", in *Combating Piracy and Ship Robbery*, edited by Ahmad and Ogawa, p. 11; Samuel Pyeatt Menefee, "Crossing the Line?: Maritime Violence, Piracy, Definitions and International Law", in *Combating Piracy and Ship Robbery*, edited by Ahmad and Ogawa, p. 66.

38. Adam J. Young and Mark J. Valencia, "Conflation of Piracy and Terrorism in Southeast Asia: Rectitude and Utility", *Contemporary Southeast Asia* 25, no. 2 (2003): 276.

39. Ahmad Reme, "Pirates and terrorists not natural allies", *Straits Times Interactive*, 29 June 2004, http://straitstimes.com (accessed 29 June 2004).

40. Ibid.

41. Young and Valencia, "Conflation of Piracy", p. 276.

42. Ibid., p. 272.

43. Aviva Freudmann, "Scotland Yard Links Increase in Piracy to Organized Crime", *Journal of Commerce*, 1 February 1999, sec. Maritime, p. 2B.

44. T. Yulianti, "Bajak Laut" [Pirates], *Suara Pembaruan Daily*, 13 June 2003, p. 2 of 4, printout from online (accessed 27 March 2004), available at http://mail2.factsoft.de/pipermail/national/2002-June/005671.html.

45. Liss, "Maritime Piracy", pp. 52–68.

46. Abhyankar, "Piracy and Ship Robbery", p. 31.

47. See Chapter 3 under the section heading Patronage of Piracy, subheading Organized Crime on p. 75, for further discussion of this high-end organized piracy.

48. See, for example, Abhyankar, "Piracy and Ship Robbery", pp. 30–31, for a discussion of the attack on the *MV Marta* involving the theft of $2 million

of tin plate, and see also discussion of the *Alondra Rainbow, Petro Ranger,* and *Tenyu* later in this text (Chapter 3).

49. Liss, "Maritime Piracy", p. 61; Eric Hobsbawm, *Bandits* (New York: Pantheon Books, 1981).

50. Maritime security is rather self-explanatory as security concerns related to the maritime realm. However, the other terms may not be as familiar. GAP is a term designating those security threats stemming from non-state actors and non-governmental processes and organizations that exist in the "grey areas" of states where state control is not fully realized (Peter Chalk, *Non-Military Security and Global Order* [New York: St. Martin's Press, LLC, 2000], pp. 2–3). Transnational crime is simply criminal activity that crosses international borders and is therefore largely beyond the control of any one specific nation. A "non-traditional security threat", as it was described in neo-realist security literature during the Cold War, was a security threat that was not an immediate risk of causing full-scale war between nations and therefore warranted less attention. Transnational crime and GAP (in which piracy could go under either term) would fit under that rubric.

51. See almost any historical work cited in this book for examples where disciplinary limits have necessarily cut off applying historical accounts to contemporary phenomena; it is simply outside the scope and aim of these works.

52. Michael Aung-Thwin, "Spirals in Early Southeast Asian and Burmese History", *Journal of Interdisciplinary History* XXI, no. 4 (Spring 1991): 592.

53. See, in particular, James Warren, "A Tale of Two Centuries", ARI Working Thesis, no. 2, June 2003 (accessed 27 March 2004), available at http://www.ari.nus.edu.sg/pub/wps2003.htm; and Ger Teitler, "Piracy in Southeast Asia: A Historical Comparison", *MAST* 1, no. 1 (2002): 67–83, online edition, http://www.marecentre.nl/mast/mastnewvol1.1.html (accessed February 2004).

54. Thomson, *Mercenaries, Pirates, and Sovereigns*, p. 54.

55. Ibid., pp. 8, 41–42, 54.

56. Muthiah Alagappa, "Introduction", in *Politcal Legitimacy in Southeast Asia,* edited by Muthiah Alagappa (Stanford: Stanford University Press, 1995), p. 2; Micheal Leifer, *Dilemmas of Statehood in Southeast Asia* (Vancouver: University of British Columbia Press, 1972), p. 105; Leslie Green, *The Authority of the State* (Oxford. Clarendon Press, 1988), p. 1.

57. Alagappa, "Introduction", in *Political Legitimacy*, p. 3.

2

Historical Piracy in Southeast Asia

This chapter will introduce, discuss, and reconstruct understandings of various phenomena in Southeast Asia under the Western rubric of "piracy". This is problematic as the word *piracy* has been used historically to describe everything from enemy combatants in war to common criminals. Piracy should not be thought of as static, but as a concept given to change over time and through experience; as Campo has described it "a concept in development."[1] However, analysing different understandings of piracy and how they have changed over time and place provides a way to cut through some of the biases in the use of the term.[2]

First, a pre-European understanding of piracy will be established through brief discussions of historic piracy, paying attention to how the term *piracy* was applied and constructed, as well as what roles piracy played in a Southeast Asian context. To illustrate these traditional understandings of piracy in maritime Southeast Asia and the dynamics of change, several case studies focusing on the eighteenth and nineteenth centuries will be discussed. First, Bugis raiding/piracy in the Malay world, then Vietnamese/Chinese piracy will be discussed, followed by a look at raiding/piracy in the Malay world centred on Riau and the maritime polities in the surrounding straits and seas reaching back to antiquity, but again focusing on the nineteenth century, will be discussed. Next, Iban raiding/piracy primarily on the west coast of Borneo will be examined, and finally, the Iranun, centred on Jolo and the Sulu Sea, will be discussed.

These understandings of piracy will provide historical context for piracy in Southeast Asia, emphasizing the role of political instability, economic patterns, and the endemic and intrinsic nature of piracy, highlighting the structural and cyclic roots of piracy in the region. Following the case studies, the interaction between European and Southeast Asian understandings of piracy will be looked at. Finally, a closing section will highlight the causative factors of historical piracy, particularly in relation to its interactions with European imperialism and colonialism. This will provide grounds for comparison of the success and problems of colonial suppression of piracy with causative factors of contemporary piracy, and issues facing contemporary states in addressing piracy.

LOCAL UNDERSTANDINGS OF PIRACY

A useful way to organize the various historic practices and understandings of piracy in Southeast Asia is offered by Campo in a typology of historical piracy. Campo breaks piracy into two broad categories, economic and political. He further divides the economic aspects of piracy into parasitic and predatory piracy, while dividing the political aspects of piracy into power-holders and power-seekers.[3] Parasitic piracy is simply feeding off trade that is passing by, generally opportunistic in nature, while predatory piracy is organized raiding and plundering, essentially state-sponsored. On the political side, piracy conducted by power-holders was an aspect of maintaining power, a rather business-like way to control trade and wealth, giving legitimacy to these practices.[4] As an extension of this, both parasitic and predatory piracy could give rise to disenfranchised political elements or competitors; power-seekers that often engaged in piracy as well.[5] True to real life, however, this typology like the one offered earlier for contemporary piracy is not set in stone, as agents could fluidly migrate across the spectrum as opportunity and specific circumstances dictated.

Even before documentary evidence becomes available, these practices may have been an element of some ancient maritime peoples' survival strategies. Very early archaeological evidence points towards a variety of peoples who lived along the coastal fringes in the region, exploiting a diversity of ecological micro-niches, such as estuarine, reef, deep sea, and even limited land-based agricultural environments, as part of a broad-based survival economy.[6] There have been people moving across the waterscape as long as there have been people and boats in the region.[7] This maritime adaptation continues on through history and becomes more evident as documentary sources become available. Whatever the shape, trade has been important to early maritime Southeast Asian societies at least since approximately 500 BCE to 200 CE when international trade goods including bronze artifacts, various kinds of beads, ceramics, and coins from the Mediterranean, Middle East, China, and India begin to appear throughout the region.[8] Given the early importance of maritime-adapted survival strategies, including commerce, while only speculative, it seems likely given the important roles that predatory maritime activities would play later, that they may have played a role in this early survival economy.

As documentary evidence becomes available it is clear that predatory maritime activities did exist early on as foreign accounts of some of these activities suggest, although it is questionable if any of the early authors directly witnessed an actual attack. These practices are described as "piracy", or at least that is the English translation of the Chinese and Arabic sources. In the early fifth century CE, Shih Fa-Hsien (the Buddhist "Illustrious in Law") travelled through the Strait of Malacca, returning to China from the holy centres of Buddhism in India, and noted of his passage "This sea is infested with pirates, to meet whom is death."[9] From the latter eighth or early ninth century an account compiled by Chia-Tan describes a particular Southeast Asian kingdom as a place where "the inhabitants are mostly pirates."[10] The literal meanings of the characters translated as "pirate" in both these accounts are ambiguous, but their context on the water suggests the idea of piracy.[11] Ibn Battutah, writing in the mid-fourteenth century, in one passage mentions junks getting ready for "piratical raids, and also to deal with any junks that might attempt to resist their exactions, for they exact tribute on each junk [calling at that place]."[12] Unfortunately, these historical forms of piracy were only sporadically documented by foreigners passing through Southeast Asia, each with their own religious, economic, and political agendas, with their own unique way of making sense of what they saw and translating it into their own languages. This complicates efforts to understand what roles piracy played in these early times and how it was conceived.

As local documents and European accounts of predatory maritime activities become more widely available in the fifteenth and sixteenth centuries, local understandings and practices of piracy come into sharper focus. For instance, the Malay word *perompak*, which Trocki elucidates as "wanderers and renegades who included hereditary outlaw bands with no fixed abode",[13] suggests an ambiguous status of power-seekers or even power-holders who are engaging in predatory and/or parasitic piracy beyond the mien of legitimate power structures. Where as the Malay *anak raja* (child of a king or ruler) describes a phenomenon where largely through raiding these princes could gain a following by seeking their fortunes at sea, and eventually even form their own state.[14] This was a way of accumulating power that eventually could be translated into legitimacy. When predatory maritime activities occurred beyond the control of a leader they were considered illegitimate piracy, but if under the auspices of a leader it was legitimate raiding, akin to privateering in a Western context. This was a fluid distinction though, as the life of La Ma'dukelleng Arung Sikang suggests. Described as a "prince of pirates" (raja bajak laut) by some sources, who became the ruler of the Buginese state of Wajo in southern Sulawesi in the late sixteenth to early seventeenth centuries,[15] La Ma'dukelleng illustrates another option where if predatory forays were successful and the raider gained enough power and/or reputation, they could demand entry into existing power structures. The ability to enforce legitimacy was an important distinction where similar practices could be piracy or raiding, illegitimate or legitimate, depending on where, when and who was engaging in them.

In the pre-European Philippines raiding was

> "The most celebrated form of ... warfare ...," called *mangayaw*, a word found in all the major languages of the Philippines, and these "... raiders were regarded as popular heroes and enjoyed inter-island reputations ... Their exploits became the stuff of local legend, and the most famous among them were ... worthy of being memorialized in ... heroic epics ...".[16]

It was normally the most respected warriors and leaders of traditional societies engaged in a competitive prestige system who participated in maritime raiding, not the wretched poor or hardened criminals typically associated with historic European piracy in the Atlantic and Caribbean.[17] Raiding/piracy was a part of the social fabric and accordingly interacted with politics, economics, and society at large. These heroes like La Ma'dukelleng, and the exploits that would earn a Filipino a place in an epic narrative, convey not only a sense of legitimacy in some cases, but of renowned and heroic stature. The myriad of words and understandings, as well as evidence of early maritime adaptations, further suggest an antiquity of predatory maritime activities beyond what scant document sources reveal. Furthermore, new words for piracy emerging out of the eighteenth and nineteenth centuries like *Illanun*, or *Lanun*, describing the exploits and style of particular raiders, suggests both a diversity and dynamism of practice.[18]

These understandings of Southeast Asian maritime predatory activities were of course further changed as the European presence in the region altered trading patterns and provoked dramatic changes in the socio-political make up of the region.[19] Through the processes of imperialism and colonialism, European concepts of piracy of the time were laid over local traditions, criminalizing traditional maritime predatory activities. However, as Tarling cautioned forty-one years ago on p. 1 "the concept of 'piracy' which carries from its European context certain standards of meaning and overtones ... render inexact its application even to ostensibly comparable Asian phenomenon."[20] The word "piracy" has been used to describe varying dynamic traditional practices spanning at least 1,500 years in Southeast Asia.

While there are many layers of labels and translations that have accumulated over the centuries and millennia, it seems clear that historic manifestations of piracy have existed in maritime Southeast Asia at least since there were people to record it, and as suggested above likely existed prior to that despite there being no literate society to document it. These practices were heterogeneous, encompassing a broad range of socio-political-cultural motives, and an equally diverse range of actual practice; and formed an intrinsic part of the socio-cultural-political matrix of many maritime peoples in the region.

CASE STUDIES

Bugis

By the seventeenth century the Bugis already had frequent contact with the Malay world, centred on the Strait of Malacca, as the Buginese were renowned traders and seafarers, whose services Malay kings had sought over the years.[21] In the mid to late seventeenth century, however, this contact increased dramatically as Buginese refugees fled from civil wars and conflict with the Dutch that raged in southern Sulawesi.[22] Buginese leaders sought refuge unsuccessfully in East Java and Sumbawa,[23] among other places where close contact with existing polities did not accord them the independence they wanted. By the mid-eighteenth century many Bugis had continued on to the Malay world, where unpopulated areas provided suitable circumstances to set up independent polities.[24] Many of these leaders in an effort to survive and expand their influence, lacking direct kinship or political ties to the region, resorted to familiar practices of raiding and piracy, putting them in the power-seeker/parasitic category. These activities served to disrupt regional trade, bringing them to the notice of local rulers and the Dutch. The Dutch were not keen on the Buginese moving into this region, as they were bitter and feared enemies from years of war in Sulawesi, but not wanting to commit the funds and not wanting to further involve themselves in regional politics they were not willing to address these incursions. Furthermore, the local states were also unable or unwilling to repulse the Buginese. In some cases local rulers made use of the Buginese and their seafaring/fighting skills, involving them in local disputes and eventually ensconcing them in regional politics. By the mid to late eighteenth century the Buginese had established themselves as part of the legitimate power structure of the region, and much of their energy turned to protecting and facilitating the trade that they once had preyed upon, now that they had a stake in it.[25]

From the brief look at the Bugis and their entry into the Malay world in the seventeenth and eighteenth centuries we see the importance of political disruptions and mass movements of sea people in creating an environment for piracy to emerge beyond the control of regional powers. The Bugis entry into the Malay world also shows that a lack of co-operation among regional powers, in part due to their relative instability as well as their choice in prioritizing issues, was partly to blame. The Bugis are also a good example of how historically piracy was part of a cycle of power as it broke down and was built up again.

Vietnamese/Chinese

The Vietnamese port town of Chiang-p'ing, located on the border between Vietnam and China, during the late eighteenth and early nineteenth centuries became the hub of one of the largest eruptions of piracy in the region's history. Far from the respective imperial capitals at Hue and Beijing, this border region was an ideal incubator for piracy. The coastal tracts of this region, typical of much of maritime Southeast Asia, are scattered with hundreds of islands that are connected by an intricate network of waterways, and by the ocean further out, where coastal peoples, petty traders and predominantly fisher folk, sought their livelihoods. Those people who lived in these areas were generally poor and existed on the margins of society, having been dislocated and ousted from the land by a mixture of runaway landlordism and other endemic sources of poverty, or were maritime peoples who had made their lives there for centuries. In China and Vietnam, owning land meant having wealth and status, so that coastal fringe areas "attracted those who could make it no where else in society".[26]

This region also had easy access to major shipping routes heading for southern China's major ports, which either passed through the network of islands and waterways, or passed just offshore of these areas. During this time there was an increasing amount of trade associated with the expanding European commerce with China (British demand for tea being one of the key driving forces), which was also stimulating raiding practices in the southern Philippines at the same time. This expanding trade provided a plethora of available targets for local pirates.

Additionally, restrictions issued by the Chinese government served to stimulate illegal trade activities that increased the involvement of people in illegal activities, blending in with the area's other maritime pursuits. This in part also provided the groundwork for land-based networks that provided markets for pirated goods as well as supplies for the pirates themselves. Piracy had consistently existed to some degree in this area, where the weight of poverty blurred lines of legality and illegality, and "for some, piracy was an extension of [those] endeavors in an environment where water was ubiquitous, and the knowledge of how to get around on it universal. In a region virtually outside government control, piracy was a plausible income-generating option."[27]

These coastal tracts were both psychologically and physically beyond the pale of the states that claimed these waters. They were in a border region where imperial authority largely faded out, and with little or no effort or interest in extending it to the water world beyond.[28] Neither the Chinese or Vietnamese states had successfully incorporated the maritime peoples living on their mutual borders. When piracy flourished, states were not able to offer their maritime peoples sufficient incentive to remain in the state.

This area possessed a latent capacity and potential for piratical activity, and only required a stimulus to push it beyond low-level endemic piracy, to a highly organized business. This stimulus came from the Tay-son rebellion in Vietnam in the late eighteenth century. The Tay-son forces took advantage of the availability of large numbers of Chinese and Vietnamese pirates/maritime peoples in the border region between Vietnam and China, using them as privateers in their navy. The pirates/ privateers, quick to seize the opportunity, were happy to oblige Tay-son's needs. Pirates would be outfitted by the Vietnamese and turned loose, returning to Chinese waters to plunder the coast and passing trade. They would take these goods back to Vietnam, to towns like Chiang-ping, where the Tay-son provided a safe harbour and would share part of the profits, and convey title and rank to these Chinese pirate entrepreneurs.[29] This would place them in the parasitic/power-seeker category of piracy as they were engaged in trying to establish the Tay-son as rulers. Initially, even with Ch'ing aid the ruling Le Emperor in Vietnam could not hold back the Tay-son rebellion, and they eventually succeeded to the point where they were able to place a ruler, Quang Trung, on the throne, and in 1788 he was recognized as the King of Annam.[30] However, through the changing fortunes of war the Tay-son by the last years of the eighteenth century were eventually defeated, and their navy, largely composed of Chinese pirates, now highly organized under several very capable leaders, moved back into Chinese waters.

These pirate/privateer groups suffered great losses while supporting the Tay-son, and back in China they fought among themselves. However, in 1805 seven pirate leaders formed a confederation that would be the dominate power-holder in southern China for the rest of the decade, and in 1807 this pirate confederation could boast in one of its fleets (the Red Flag Fleet) some 300 junks and 20,000 to 40,000 men![31] Under the organization of the confederacy piracy became a big, organized business, and at one point the pirates invaded the Pearl River, threatening the major trading port of Canton. Extensive coastal networks formed to supply the pirates with food, and provide markets for their goods, which the Ch'ing were powerless to stop. At this point piracy in the region moved into the power-holder category as they dominated the coast, and fluidly moved between parasitic piracy, taking advantage of the passing trade, to predatory piracy, actively raiding and pillaging parts of the coast and merchant fleets.

Internal problems beset the Ch'ing as several rebellions sprung up at the end of the eighteenth century, taking years to finally put down,[32] and thus the massive organization of pirates was left largely unhindered in their ambitions. Eventually, after many failed, uncommitted attempts, with help from British and Portuguese forces, internal dissension within the pirate ranks, and outright bribery of their leaders,[33] the Ch'ing government saw the confederacy come to an end in 1809.

This Vietnamese/Chinese case study of piracy demonstrates that piracy frequently emerged at the margins of states, both the physical margins of land (versus the sea) and territorial authority, as well as psychological margins of terra firma based identities. At these margins are often marginal peoples, coastal dwellers with maritime skills living in chronic poverty with little or no access to the expanding trade passing by their doorstep, and what opportunities they do have are cut into by restrictive trade policies of the landed state. This creates a latent capacity for piracy, where its presence is endemic and only needs a spark to trigger its expansion. In this case political instability and resulting state-sponsored piracy allowed the expansion and organization of piracy in the region.

Malay

Malay piracy in this case study focuses on the nineteenth century, looking at the effects of political and economic cycles in the region, but also reaches back into antiquity and as such will include most categories from the earlier typology. In the literature, Malay[34] raiding and piracy is recorded in association with some of the oldest known polities in the region. The Malay heartland between Borneo and Aceh, centred on the Riau Archipelago and the Strait of Malacca, has been the focus of epigraphic and textual investigations exploring processes of maritime state formation.[35] In these processes, trade, regional and international, has emerged as a key mechanism to stimulating state formation, and piracy was an important aspect of this development.

Srivijaya in the seventh to eleventh centuries, and later Malay states such as Melaka, Aceh, Johor, Riau, and Pasai appear to have been based on a system of charismatic leadership, or in the terms of O. W. Wolters a "man of prowess", where the personal nature of the leader was the attractive and binding force of his followers.[36] From this central leader power radiated outward, diminishing as it expanded, forming a territorially transient polity without fixed borders. Furthermore, the basis of this loose territoriality was predicated on controlling people rather than realty. This was a consequence extending from a low population density characteristic of the region until recent times. Lewis writes:

> Population and wealth were the denominators and wealth often dictated population, for Malay demography was notoriously fluid...The ruler of a rich port could attract followers if his wealth was cannily distributed. Wealth in itself was an attraction, for its possession implied an almost mystical power. And the accumulation of wealth in the straits of Malacca was tied to the control of an attractive and prosperous port[37]

Raiding, or piracy, functioned as one way to amass this wealth. Wealth in this circumstance was understood as more than simply material possessions to pay for labour. Wealth was more a symbol of prestige than any kind of representation of purchase power, lending authority to a ruler's assertions of power. The low population density coupled with the high mobility of maritime people, required that a leader treat his followers and tributaries with some amount of leniency and respect, or they could move and find a better offer.

Wealth should also be thought of in terms of people, and not just willing followers, for frequently the aim of raids was the taking of slaves to either sell, or to bolster the number of followers.[38] This aspect of raiding had particular importance for the Iranun to be discussed later on. Raiding in this scenario plays two important roles, it accumulates wealth, and thereby ritual potency, enhancing a leader's "prowess", and conversely it reduces the wealth of competitors, negatively affecting their leadership position and the integrity of their polity.

A ruler's power was ritualized through oath taking ceremonies, and through the use of imprecations threatening various gruesome illnesses or death if these oaths were not maintained, rather than through direct threat of physical force. Additionally, a leader could assert influence and legitimacy by restricting distribution of specific prestige goods like bronzes, agate or carnelian beads, and ceramics, which accorded ritual "prowess",[39] thus controlling the distribution of wealth and power. The state could expect loyalty as long as they provided economic or social opportunity (honour, glory, rank, and title), and maintained their authority and legitimacy (thereby preserving their potency). When the state could no longer maintain these relationships, due to shifts in international trade, because of successful raids by competitors (as may have been the case with Srivijaya and raids from the Chola Empire in southern India),[40] or simply because new leadership did not have the same charismatic power, maritime peoples spun out from their orbit of control, turning to alternative sources of patronage and opportunity such as piracy. Whereas before, these peoples might have protected trade, pacifying regions to facilitate trade for a given state, they now exploited that trade directly through parasitic and predatory raiding rather than benefiting from the central leader's redistribution of goods.[41]

Control of economic processes has been important for raiding/piracy in Southeast Asia for 1,500 years or more, as the region has been a hub and intersection of global trade since the first millennium CE.[42] By the time of Srivijaya in the ninth century, international trade and exchange, including in religion, art and political structures, as well as commercial goods, was already the life blood of maritime political structures in the Malay world. This global exchange of goods and ideas drove the maritime economy of Southeast Asia, and the structure of piracy changed dependent on this trade and the ability of states to control and redistribute it.

The manpower associated with these practices came from various labour pools of sea-oriented peoples, such as various groups of *Orang Laut* and the Bugis whom a leader could induce to his cause when need be. Except for a few of the elite sea peoples who were directly linked to certain polities, however, most groups were not full-time raiders and had to make ends meet in a variety of other ways. They did not conveniently hoist a black flag to communicate their affiliations or intentions. In fact many raiders were only active when the fishing season was done, or when a particular opportunity presented itself. For many groups piracy was only a part-time occupation, another facet of a broad-based survival strategy, and commerce was another resource to be exploited. The same people on the same boat could be variously engaged in collecting trade goods like sea slugs, bird nests, fishing for their own consumption or to sell, trading other merchant's goods, and/ or raiding. Part of the frustration of attempts to suppress piracy by colonial powers was this very ambiguity, where people who were raiders or pirates where not always so, and colonial powers often had little idea who was a "pirate" and who was not. The British at one point began firing at any vessel with a certain kind of sail that they associated with "pirate" craft.[43] Piracy was a fluid part of a survival strategy and difficult to nail down to any one person or group.

The cyclic nature of piracy based on economic trends, however, was tempered through the cultural links and oaths of clients and patrons that superseded material goods. Various groups of *Orang Laut*, for example, maintained loyal ties to the lineage of rulers stemming from the royal line of Srivijaya, continuing to Melaka, Johor, and Malay Riau. This does not mean that the *Orang Laut* never engaged in piracy as long as these rulers existed, but once power was reconstituted they would respond to these ancient relationships, recognizing their ties to that particular royal line.[44]

From the seventeenth to nineteenth centuries Europeans increasingly impacted these cyclic processes, as their trade competition often involved disruptions of local power structures, such as the Portuguese capture of Melaka in 1511, and British involvement and imperial expansion in the Malay world in the eighteenth and nineteenth centuries, which frequently involved suppressing Malay "piracy". These changes disrupted the cyclic reformation of power structures in much of the Malay world. Piracy could be a reconstitutive energy as intense rivalry and competition eventually settled into more stable structures, but European involvement short-circuited this reformative cycle, leaving only the chaos. In the literature this phenomenon became known as the "decay theory".[45] Initial disruptions led to a fragmentation of power, yet at the same time international trade was booming, both from the spice trade in the sixteenth and seventeenth centuries, and increasingly from the China trade in the eighteenth and nineteenth centuries, creating economic opportunities for those who could take advantage. In this way wealth began to accrue to individual leaders, rather than to larger political centres to be redistributed, creating a proliferation of helter-skelter competition for resources, frequently beyond the control of established, but fading, polities.

The Malay case study provides insight into what roles piracy/raiding played in maritime societies, also building on examples from the definitions section. This case study highlights piracy as part of a broad-based survival strategy, with roots possibly stretching deep into pre-history, intrinsic to the maritime region. It is clear that piracy was not just an enterprise of desperate and hardened criminals, although it certainly had aspects that were considered illegitimate, but rather it was part of the socio-political-economic system that underlay the development of states and regional power structures dependent on passing trade. This case study also shows how the charismatic leader was at the centre of power structures, attracting and keeping critical manpower through a ritualized redistribution of goods. This created prestige, power and potency for the leader, thus cementing the legitimacy of loyalties and oaths. Malay piracy also demonstrates important linkages between the control of trade, political stability and piracy. States and regional power structures needed to maintain the loyalties of maritime peoples, and any destabilization of the systems that made this possible could result in increases of piracy.

Iban

According to the oral traditions of the Saribas Iban (Iban of the Saribas River), two to four generations before the arrival of the British and the Brookes in Borneo, the main concern of these people was migration and opening up of new lands, emphasizing local affairs and contacts with close neighbours.[46] Opening new lands was not an easy job, and accordingly a prestigious accomplishment; "the pioneer cultivator of old jungle, like the successful warrior, is a figure of immense prestige in Iban society."[47] When this migration period into Sarawak was still relatively new for Iban peoples, and there were lots of "open" territory (although much of it was occupied by other groups who were killed or absorbed by the Iban), sea raiding was not as prevalent. However, by the mid-nineteenth century things began to change.

Clues to the motivations and forces driving this explosive period of Iban raiding in the mid-nineteenth century come from oral accounts of the Iban themselves. As these accounts indicate, migration and opening new lands was important, so that by the mid-nineteenth century there were fewer lands to open, due to earlier migrations and increasing contact with other peoples. This may have led to increasing population densities and conflict for resources, for Iban disputes often circled around access to important resources like fruit and honey trees, bird nests, or about territorial encroachment.[48] Additionally, as virgin jungle became less available a shift in acquiring prestige happened, from emphasizing the pioneer to emphasizing the warrior, and defending territory already cleared from encroachment. Saribas accounts discuss an important warrior, Unggang, who after receiving a message from a divine warrior patroness, constructed a large war boat with which he went to the mouth of the river to defend against *Illanun* raids, and all other strangers entering that part of the South China Sea.[49] In this way defending against territorial encroachment and raids brought Iban warriors to the coast where they became embroiled in regional political affairs in a distinctly Iban manner, and at the same time this provided an outlet for internal pressures.

At this time Iban chiefs began taking Malay titles like *Temenggong* and *Orang Kaya* that did not appear in the past, signifying changes in the political life of the Iban, as they became more involved in Malay politics, while their social structure remained fairly constant.[50] These changes in Iban political life in the nineteenth century developed as they enmeshed themselves in a complex network of long-distance inter-tribal warfare (as compared to the local nature of conflict and interaction previously), connected with local Malay chiefs at various river mouths, the British in the form of Brookes and his drive to carve out a personal empire, and the weak but still prestigious Brunei Sultanate.[51] The Iban raids attracted British animosity and initiated punitive attacks from war ships like the *H.M.S. Dido*, under the command of Henry Keppel, in an effort to "suppress piracy". It is clear from Keppel's and Brooke's own accounts these expeditions were instrumental in installing Brooke as the "White Rajah" of Sarawak, besides suppressing Iban "piracy".[52]

Certain Malay chiefs, ostensibly under the control of the Brunei Sultanate were extending their power at the expense of the Iban, as symbolized, figuratively and perhaps literally, by Iban accounts of unfair taxation carried out through deceptive rice baskets that could hold more than they were supposed to.[53] The Brunei Sultanate in its weakened condition was powerless to stop local chiefs from accruing wealth to themselves rather than passing it along to the political centre. This build up of wealth outside the centre fractured political power in the region.

In turn these abuses, or perceived abuses, stimulated retaliatory raids from the Iban, which in turn stimulated attacks from Malay chiefs and the Brookes in alliance with Brunei. In this way inter-tribal warfare, which was an intrinsic feature of many groups of Iban at this time,[54] became much more regionalized and pronounced than before. The Brookes and Malay chiefs took advantage of inter-tribal rivalries, just as Iban groups took advantage of Malay and Brookes' political intrigues, to recruit help for their attacks in furthering their own political ambitions. This process stimulated greater antagonisms between Iban groups and promoted an escalation of raiding. As rival tribes sought or were defending their power, predatory raiding played an important part in these struggles.

Iban piracy/raiding is not entirely dissimilar to Malay models of raiding. They both emerged out of the same political-economic turmoil at this period. The fundamental reasons for Iban raiding were quite similar to Malay raiding practices, in that it was an expression of competition and prestige, but whereas Malay raiding was often involved in larger scale political processes of state competition, Iban raiding was more intimate, being part of a smaller more personal political system. Illustrative of this difference is the "booty" sought by each group. Malay raiding, even when punitive in nature or part of warfare, had as a goal the accumulation of material goods — gold, cloth, beads, ceramics, people — even if used for largely ritualized purposes. Iban raiding also sought material goods, including people, for prestige, but often in the form of heads.

Among many groups of Iban, most notably in nineteenth century European accounts of the Iban peoples along the Saribas and Skrang rivers, head-hunting was an integral part of life. Similar to what Iban oral traditions record, Ulla Wagner points out that competition for land and resources induced groups to wage war,[55] from which heads were often taken as trophies of prestige and spiritual potency. As part of this prestige system, Wagner notes that some Iban tell the story that in order to obtain status and to attract a suitable spouse,[56] and follow the *adat*, or traditions of the past,[57] head taking was very important. For example, head taking fulfilled important mortuary roles, as Wagner relates that when a kinsman was killed a head needed to be procured as retaliation to fulfil a moral obligation.[58] Related to this, Gomes notes that in order to break the mourning period for a deceased relative, a head must be gotten.[59] All of these reasons for head-hunting, and accordingly for participating in raiding expeditions, were integral to the status of individuals and to the smooth functioning of the local community. The emphasis on head taking in the nineteenth century can also been seen as a reflection of the shift from pioneering to raiding in response to the internal pressures of population growth and expansion.

Iban piracy was at once very much involved in the political and economic changes taking place in Southeast Asia, but at the same time was an extension of their traditional practices. While Malay piracy seems to have been in part the result of political decay of traditional polities, Iban raiding was part of a socio-political expansion of the Iban, an extension of a process started several generations prior to British incursions.

This Iban case study serves two main purposes: one to show another example of how raiding was important to pre-European peoples, particularly one that contrasts with all the other cases being very "traditional" and locally motivated; and second to show how changes in local circumstances can interact with wider regional circumstances in spurring an increase in piracy.

Iranun

The Sulu Sultanate, using the extensive raiding of groups like the Iranun,[60] came to its peak influence and power in the later eighteenth and nineteenth centuries, as the burgeoning China trade made them a centre of international trade. In many ways they represent the pinnacle of raiding as an economic and political tool. While still very much grounded in traditional practices that place great prestige on raiding, not dissimilar to aspects of Iban and Malay forms of raiding, the Iranun model can be seen as an indigenous development of raiding in a modern, capitalist economy. The Iranun raids provided goods, wealth, and particularly slaves, the means of producing wealth, the backbone of the economy for the Sulu Sultanate. Ironically, it was also Buginese and Chinese traders' demand for slaves, to feed the expanding colonial empires' need for labour, which helped create a market for slave raiding that was often carried out in their own territories.[61]

According to James Warren, the author of two major volumes, and several smaller articles and monographs on the Iranun and their close cousins ethnically and occupationally the Balangingi,[62] the Iranun were launched into large-scale maritime raiding as the result of an act of God. Not untypical of the region a volcano near their homeland in southwestern Mindanao erupted and devastated much of their lands.[63] The Iranun were coastally adapted peoples, but their numbers extended landward where they were also farmers. However, as a result of the volcanic eruption thousands of Iranun fled the interior for the coast of Mindanao and beyond, thus forcing these people to use what skills they had to eke out a living from the sea. This was the initial push that forced these people, or helped them choose, to rely on raiding as a means of support.

Following the prevailing monsoon winds, these raids swept out across most of maritime Southeast Asia, extending from Sumatra, the Malay Peninsula, the Gulf of Thailand, the coast of Vietnam, and to the waters of New Guinea and the Moluccas, including the heavily raided coasts of the central Philippines. The primary objectives of these raids were slaves. Slaves played an important role in the social hierarchy of Sulu, as it did in other associated cultures of the pre-Spanish Philippines.[64] However, in response to the burgeoning China trade of the times, in which Sulu was an important supplier of trade goods to European and American traders who then used these goods to trade in China, the Sultanate's demand for slaves increased dramatically. With this increased demand the social prestige associated with owning slaves also increased, solidifying this trend into cultural practice. The growing capitalist market in China was stimulating Sulu to expand its enterprise.

As part of this system raids were carried out along strict hierarchical lines, based on a system of rigid social status focusing on individual leaders who commanded personal followers. Leaders of expeditions would often be high-ranking members of society, and the raids themselves if successful allowed for some social mobility. Ships would be outfitted as an investment, with the wealthier elements of society investing in the goods and labour needed to carry out a raid in exchange for a percentage of the profits.[65] This state-sponsored raiding was vital to Sulu, and nominally the Iranun were under the authority of the Sulu Sultanate in this system; meaning when called to his service they would answer. However, the raids stimulated by the Sultanate were only marginally controlled by the state itself, and they often took on a life of their own. Iranun often independently organized and outfitted their own expeditions, and only paid their patrons what was their contractual due. The system benefited the Sultanate, but it was also beyond their direct control. The Iranun had independent communities spread throughout the archipelago that acted as bases for raiding expeditions.[66] These widespread communities and base camps made extensive raiding possible, acting as resupply points and safe havens. They adhered to an internal hierarchy where the Sultanate was in theory the top of the hierarchy, but often a very distant figure.

Eventually, these communities became targets for colonial powers and their local allies suppression of piracy. Beyond their home territory in northern Borneo and the Sulu Sea these communities were destroyed with their inhabitants resettled as farmers, thus effectively curtailing their raiding activities in these areas.[67] In fact it was the curtailing of the Iranun raids in the mid and latter part of the nineteenth century that signalled the decline of the Sulu Sultanate. The China trade was increasingly dominated by Western powers and moved away from Sulu, in part because of effective blockades by the Spanish, and changing priorities for English and American traders that had frequented Sulu, as well as direct attacks by regional colonial powers on the Sultanate. As a result Sulu faded into ignominy by the twentieth century, although notably, the Sultanate retained enough autonomy to conduct a separate treaty with the United States following the Spanish American War at the turn of the century.[68]

The efficiency and ruthlessness of Iranun raids made them infamous throughout maritime Southeast Asia, with the southerly monsoons that come in September being called the "pirate wind" because it brought these raiders down into the archipelago. Part of the success of this system was its flexibility and fluidity. Raids were characterized by temporary alliances of co-operation, sometimes from several settlements and often across ethnic groups, from which large expeditions could be assembled.[69] Raiding groups in Southeast Asia generally used a wide variety of shallow draft sailing vessels that were also subsidiarily powered by oars. These vessels had an enormous range in size, some of which like the *joanga* in the nineteenth century, were approximately 100 to 130 feet in length, powered by 100 to 150 men, mounting 8 to 10 bronze and iron swivel cannons on the starboard and port decks.[70] Likewise the composition of ships' crew was often quite diverse, being composed of Iranun, Iban, Papuans, Visayans and other people from the Philippine Archipelago, Malays, whomever had been captured and forced into service, or had voluntarily joined the expedition.[71] Warren notes that it was often these local recruits that proved the most effective, or disastrous depending on your point of view, for they had intimate local knowledge of the waterways, reefs, shoals, holidays, and settlement patterns, which greatly facilitated raids.[72] The Iranun, like their other piratical counterparts in Southeast Asia, were not exclusively raiders, and when not in the raiding season they would often participate in collecting sea slugs, bird nests, and other natural trade goods to sell at market.[73] This fluidity and flexibility made it difficult for Europeans to target specific groups, and even if a certain group were predominantly raiders, unless they were caught in the act, it was often difficult to distinguish a peaceful group from a raiding party; they blended into the background.

The large-scale success of Iranun raids was significantly attributable to the fact that many polities in the region were in a state of decline or were structurally weak. By the late eighteenth and early nineteenth century the military and economic condition of the Philippines under Spanish rule was deteriorating, partly due to the Iranun raids themselves, and they were not able to muster the necessary funds to provide for the defence of the colony.[74] The Iranun raids, while contributing to the deterioration of the colony, were also a sign of its already impoverished, weakened condition.[75] Increasing crime rates and confrontational behaviour on land in the Philippines during the nineteenth century, suggests that raiding was not the only worry of the Spanish.[76] Villages and small towns were left virtually defenceless by the Spanish, and left to their own means they frequently had little recourse except to flee to the interior until the raiders had passed. Similarly, the Dutch were not in a position to combat the incursive raids of the Iranun in the Moluccas, the former heartland of their spice empire, during the same time-frame. For various reasons the Dutch were experiencing internal problems as their homeland was threatened and engulfed by French Napoleonic ambitions, and later their corporate structure failed and the colonial possessions of the Dutch East India company reverted to direct state control. Iranun raiding again, ironically in part stimulated by colonial demand for slaves, ravaged the islands of the eastern archipelago and essentially curtailed Dutch power in the region except for a few fortified sites.[77] Additionally, although the Iranun menace had largely subsided, from 1873 onward rebellion in Aceh was a continual drain on Dutch finances and security forces.[78] Furthermore, there was a general lack of co-operation between the Dutch and the British regarding the Iranun raids. On the one hand the British denounced Iranun raids in the Malay world and encouraged their suppression, but on the other hand they tacitly encouraged Iranun raids in the Moluccas as part of their efforts to compete with the Dutch.

In the western end of maritime Southeast Asia many areas fared little better than the Dutch or Spanish. By the late eighteenth and early nineteenth centuries the Malay world was largely fragmented into small states and polities that had difficulty mounting effective resistance to the Iranun raids. It was in part the endemic bickering and warring between polities in the region that initially brought the Iranun to the area. Their aid was sought by a local ruler to oust the Dutch from Riau, which they successfully did while plundering the island.[79] Additionally, the British creation of Singapore as a major entrepôt attracting local and international trade also attracted the Iranun to the area. From bases like Reteh, Sambas, and Tempasuk, they raided up and down the Strait of Malacca and throughout the Riau-Lingga Archipelago.[80] The British, like the local states as well as the Spanish and Dutch, were also going through turbulent times. The British, like the rest of Europe, were distracted and weakened by the Napoleonic wars, and wars in Burma as well. Eventually the Dutch, English, and to some degree the Spanish, would overcome their temporary weakened conditions and assert their control over the region once again, but this was not a quick process for the Iranun continued to plunder and raid across the archipelago until the mid-nineteenth century, and on a lesser scale until almost the end of the century.

Like the Iban, Iranun raids were deeply involved in regional politics of the times, and were associated with expanding political power, not necessarily "decaying" power, contrasting with Malay piracy in the eighteenth and nineteenth century that erupted in the wake of fragmenting political authority and burgeoning trade. Indeed the large-scale raids of the Iranun did not represent the downfall or weakening of the Sulu Sultanate, but were part of its rapid growth and prosperity. Although both Iranun and Iban took advantage of the weak conditions of regional polities, using them to their own benefits, whether for prestige, for slaves, or for heads, piracy for them was not a sign of political instability.

The Iranun case study brings out several important themes, such as the role of state support in the expansion of raiding, or piracy to those inflicted with their raids, as well as the role of states in controlling piracy, highlighting the importance of competition and co-operation of regional powers. This aspect of the Iranun case study also shows how the threat of piracy can create a justification for foreign powers to intervene in regional politics. The Iranun also provide insight into how to address the root causes of piracy, dealing with the infrastructure and socio-political-economic system that gave rise to their raids, and what allowed European powers to finally do this, emphasizing a multilateral approach, effective use of technology, and the use of local knowledge. The expansive range of the Iranun, more so than the other groups discussed, also highlights the interconnectedness of the maritime region and problems controlling maritime boundaries.

INTERACTION WITH WESTERN UNDERSTANDINGS OF PIRACY

The increase in indigenous "piracy" during the latter half of the eighteenth century and through much of the nineteenth century resulted in part from changes in the economic and political structures of maritime Southeast Asia, which had started with the Portuguese conquest of Malacca in 1511, but was also simply an extension of indigenous political, social, and cultural processes. This increase in piracy proved enormously difficult for European imperial, and then colonial powers, to control. The fragmentation of power combined with huge increases in regional trade provided ample targets for parasitic as well as state sponsored predatory raiders such as the Iranun. Raiding and piracy went virtually unchecked for almost a century as European powers struggled to overcome difficulties at home, and to find local alliances and partners that were willing to co-operate in achieving their economic and political goals in the region. Part of the problem in doing so was the slim profit margins the colonies often operated on, and colonial powers in general were not willing to commit too much effort if it upset those profit margins.[81]

Additionally, on a more technical level, despite a seemingly overwhelming advantage to European ships, as native craft were not close in size or fire power to European warships,[82] local craft had a number of advantages. Some of the advantages were their shallow drafts, important for navigating the reef strewn seascape and riverine environments, the lack of iron nails which tended to rust out quickly in the warm tropical seas, the added use of oars which could provide a needed burst of speed, or power the vessel in calm winds, and the craft were manufactured with local materials at a fraction the cost of a European vessel. The Dutch were often forced to rely on local vessels for anti-piracy uses as their own were to slow and too costly,[83] and similarly with the Spanish. These advantages helped raiders/pirates like the Iranun compete with European vessels well into the nineteenth century. However, the technical advantage swung towards the colonial powers with the development of relatively low-cost, mass-produced steam vessels. The efficiency of steam power allowed more effective patrols, even in strong ocean currents or when lacking wind, and the shallow draft of steam ships allowed them to navigate waters previously off limits,[84] bringing modern firepower to bear on raider strong holds, as well as expanding the political control of the colonial powers. The raiders and pirates were not yet capable of making use of the new technology, and so it was entirely in the advantage of the colonial states.

Firearms follow a similar story as boats, as initially in the sixteenth and early seventeenth centuries there was a rough equivalency in the quality and quantity of firearms, including heavy ordinance, available to Southeast Asian and European states.[85] Typically each European vessel could muster more and bigger cannon than could any single Southeast Asian vessel, but when beset by several native pirate craft, European vessels could still be outmanoeuvred, outgunned, or overpowered. However, over the following 250 years European firearm technology continued to advance while indigenous Southeast Asian technological capacity did not keep pace, and local demand had to increasingly rely on European supplies of arms.[86] This was not a huge problem to raiders and pirates as they had not typically produced their own munitions anyway, but rather purchased or "collected" their arms. For instance, Sulu acquired much of its arms from American traders, to the dismay of English, Spanish and Dutch authorities, as part of the China trade thriving at the time.[87] As with vessels however, local arms acquisition could not keep pace with what the colonial states could muster, and as raiding/piratical activity was reduced so too was their access to firearms.[88]

Beyond vessels and guns, information was also the key element both allowing raiders/pirates to operate and in controlling their activities. In the past, pirates/raiders and the state apparatus relied heavily upon human resources for their knowledge, as more sophisticated means were not yet available. The dissemination of this knowledge in turn also relied heavily on word of mouth, which greatly restricted its usefulness. As technical developments evolved, new methods of gathering and disseminating information became available to the colonial states that were not available to raiders/pirates. Colonial states built lighthouses and beacons in key choke points and frequented trade passages, allowing the colonial state to literally peer into the veil of darkness where smuggling and other activities contrary to the wishes of the state were taking place.[89] This technology could also be used by enterprising pirates, however, as one group figured out that where these beacons were set up trade tended to gather, so they simply set watch near the beacon.[90] Additionally, as important as the tactical advantage of steam power was in combating piracy, maybe more important was that steam power allowed the empire to expand, reaching more out-of-the-way places and speeding communications and trade; as Tagliacozzo writes: "The advent of steam aided the imperial project immeasurably, not just in Southeast Asia but in the rest of the world as well."[91] Faster still was in the latter nineteenth century, when telegraph cables were laid from the metropoles to the colonies themselves.[92] This allowed disparate parts of the state to communicate with each other, and the metropole back in Europe, in a matter of minutes rather than days, weeks, or months. The state utilized these communication networks and expanded their organization and control. Moreover, the local knowledge that was so important to the success of raiding/piracy was also eventually utilized by states seeking to control these activities. As their familiarity with the area increased, European maps got better, and more local peoples were incorporated into the state structure, and local knowledge became more widely disseminated. Places to hide or to independently organize beyond the reach of the state dwindled.

Raiding/piracy practices, however, also proved extremely flexible and adaptive to the changing capabilities of their pursuers. At their height the Iranun could muster 200 vessels or more, and similarly Iban and Malay raiders could organize massive fleets, as one reported off the coast of Borneo had "150 *bangkong* [warships] with about 2,000 or 3,000 men, with three chiefs."[93] Eventually, however, these large-scale expeditions became impractical and impossible, being highly vulnerable to mass conflicts where the advantages of modern European steam power and weapons were evident. In response to this changing situation the Iranun shifted gears towards smaller ships, smaller fleets, and more frequent raids, thus playing to their advantages and avoiding direct conflict with powerful European warships. In this way, for thirty years after the destruction of their home bases in the mid-nineteenth century, these groups could continue to carry out raids, using "hit and run" tactics where surprise and mobility let them conduct attacks often in less than an hour, providing time for escape before the authorities could respond.[94]

Eventually, by the mid- to late-nineteenth century the Dutch, British and Spanish were coming to terms carving up Southeast Asia into their respective spheres of influence, and so co-operation between the countries could grow as competition for territory lessened. It was only by this time that regional governments were thinking about how they could co-operate to suppress piracy in the region,[95] and to a large extent this concerted effort was successful.[96] By the nineteenth century, as privateering was being outlawed in Europe, the interpretation of piracy as a wholly criminal practice, involving private gains (*animo furandi*) and as an act against all humanity (*hostes humani generis*), therefore punishable by all nations, was cemented, leaving little tolerance for similar practices in Southeast Asian waters. Also, as Tarling explains at length, British territorial, political, and ultimately the desire for economic expansion in the Malay world in the nineteenth century, was frequently placed under the guise of "suppressing piracy".[97] Similarly in the Sulu Archipelago and in Mindanao the Spanish used the suppression of piracy and/or religious language to justify continued war with various Islamic rulers. The Dutch as well also frequently saw the suppression of piracy, and the resultant subjugation of local states, as a necessary step in establishing a colonial state.[98] As was the case with the British, all their acts were of course not entirely unjustified from their perspective, as local states were not free of war-like or unscrupulous behaviour even in their own socio-cultural-political terms, but there was a frequent use of suppressing piracy by extra-regional powers for larger political and economic ambitions.

Despite the persistence of indigenous practices that continued through most of the nineteenth century,[99] by the end of the century they had largely ceased. Maritime competition in the form of raiding was *de facto* eliminated, replaced by "crime" and "rebellion", acts at variance with established colonial state practices. Interaction and negotiation of maritime practice no longer focused on broad competition between rival systems, but now became a matter of what was beyond the reach and control of colonial states. European influence dramatically changed definitions of legitimacy and forever altered power structures in the region. Local states and time-honoured raiding practices would no longer be the basis of legitimacy for predatory maritime activities, as colonial powers, and their successors, the independent nation states of Southeast Asia, became the locus of power and authority in the region. Moreover, these maritime realms were increasingly relegated to the margins, as the indigenous maritime states that once competed for trade and power were conquered and/or absorbed, and colonial states were more focused on an export plantation economy rather than controlling maritime trade. Yet, piracy persisted throughout the colonial era, evolving and adapting. It is unclear how far colonial law really penetrated into the consciousness of most maritime peoples, especially since they lived at the marginal, watery edges of state control.[100] "It [piracy] just moved into the interstitial seams between the 'sinews' of state power, seeking out places and moments where such attacks had a chance of success."[101]

CAUSATIVE FACTORS OF HISTORICAL PIRACY

Historic manifestations of piracy in Southeast Asia were heterogeneous, encompassing a broad range of socio-political-cultural motives, and an equally diverse range of actual practice, which despite being translated as "piracy" bore little resemblance to European concepts of piracy. In the past, piracy was an intrinsic and/or endemic part of the socio-cultural-political matrix in much of maritime Southeast Asia. Control of passing trade and the redistribution of wealth by a charismatic leader were at the heart of systems governing political and social ties. Piracy/raiding naturally fit into this system as a way to control passing trade, compete with rivals, and win personal prestige through heroic deeds. Piracy/raiding could be both a means of protecting trade and the wealth of the state when controlled by the ruler, but could also be the means of its downfall as wealth accumulated to rival centres of power. When states and local power structures could no longer control the flow of wealth, they lost a key grip on their maritime peoples, who would then seek their own share of the wealth through piracy. As piracy proliferated beyond state control, trade would divert to rival entrepôts that could provide better security.

Particularly indicative of piracy in Southeast Asia since the arrival of Europeans are conditions of economic growth (increasing trade through the region) and political weakness and/or instability. From the sixteenth century onward, but particularly in the late eighteenth and nineteenth centuries, local and international trade increased steadily and at times exponentially as the region was directly involved in expanding and quickening global trade networks. The incursions of European powers into the trade dynamics of the region upset many long-standing balances of power, and/or quickened the natural demise of states, creating political instability among states and power structures in much of the region. As these power structures struggled to maintain or even to expand their influence, raiding and piracy became rampant in all of the forms outlined in the historic typology of piracy. All of the historic case studies bear this out. Prior to European imperialism and colonialism, indigenous maritime states would periodically experience destabilization, leading to competition for power and wealth to expand their personal prestige and influence, which in turn stimulated parasitic and predatory raiding/piracy. Eventually a coalescence of regional power structures would then reign in piracy. With the invasive and unsettling presence of European powers in the region this process was interrupted, and with the establishment of colonial states it became impossible as the process was subsumed under the term "piracy".

In the nineteenth century for the British, Dutch and Spanish, the "suppression of piracy" became a reason, and at times an excuse, to expand political and economic control over territories. This process was not uncontested, however, and European expansion in the region was frequently challenged both by competition with other states, such as the raiding of the Iranun supported under the Sulu Sultanate, and by independent agents of piracy as well.

This period is instructive because it is the first time Westphalian state structures, the forerunners of modern independent nations of Southeast Asia, tried to secure large tracts of maritime territory under their legal codes, and suppress piracy/raiding in Southeast Asia as a criminal enterprise. This had not been an issue for local power structures as piracy was an important part of their political system, and their power was based on people, not territory. Europeans became the first folks to try and police the waters of Southeast Asia.

The challenges faced by the emerging colonial powers in the latter eighteenth and first half of the nineteenth century could not be effectively met, as much of Europe was either engaged in the Napoleonic wars or recovering from the aftermath, compromising the abilities of European powers to commit ships to Southeast Asia to secure them from piracy. Following the Napoleonic wars their competition for territory and control of trade in the region escalated, reducing their willingness and ability to co-operate in addressing the common issue of piracy/raiding. Security against piracy was also hampered by tight colonial budgets whose bottom line was the profit margin. Furthermore, until later in the nineteenth century local vessels, intelligence, and tactics were able to effectively take advantage of European powers weaknesses, engaging in surprise hit-and-run tactics, attacking becalmed ships, using night raids, disguising themselves as, or truly part-timing, as fishermen, evading pursuit and capture in the shallow reefs and estuaries, and hiding out in forts and villages beyond European knowledge. The vast sea spaces where these groups could operate were beyond control, and their bases and operations were safe from interference.

By the mid-nineteenth century, however, the advantages the raiders/pirates enjoyed, and the space they operated in began to dwindle. The support they received from regional states and power structures began to be eroded as European powers, now recovering from the Napoleonic wars and fully engaged in the China tea trade, more directly sought to curtail these state's "piratical" presence. Furthermore, when colonial spheres of influence were carved out and borders were settled and direct competition between the European powers lessened, co-operation in addressing issues like piracy became a possibility. As European powers began to expand their influence, in large part thanks to technical developments in steam power, communications, and firearms, they began to incorporate local knowledge and intelligence, which provided key tactical details of pirate operations. The advances in ship design and firepower also allowed them to follow up their intelligence and destroy pirate bases, such as the raiding bases of the Iranun at Tempasuk in northern Borneo, Balangingi in the Sulu Archipelago, and on modern day Belitung and Bangka off southern Sumatra. Under colonial power all forms of predatory maritime behaviour outside their control became conflated with piracy, an enterprise that threatened the economic and political well being of the region, a crime that was *hostes humanis generis* motivated by *animo furundi*, thus illegitimate and punishable under common law and civil law codes. These developments drastically reduced the operational spaces of pirates and raiders alike, and thus they could only exist at the margins of state control, in the sinews of the new state.

These changes failed, however, to completely alter the environment that could give rise to piracy when conditions were once again ripe, i.e. the colonial powers did not fully change the socio-cultural matrix and survival strategies of maritime Southeast Asia, the roots remained entrenched at the edges of colonial state power. Thus, the hotspots of piracy today are frequently geographically coterminous with the loci of indigenous maritime power structures in the nineteenth century. Places such as the Sulu Archipelago, Riau, and much of the island-specked South China Sea that became backwaters under the new power structures, at the edge of territorially based states and on the economic and social margins. While unable to fundamentally eradicate some of the roots of piracy in the region, the colonial powers through their increasing control of the region did radically change the environment in which piracy operated, severely restricting its scope and frequency.

Notes

1. Joseph N.F.M. a Campo, "Discourse without Discussion: Representation of Piracy in Colonial Indonesia 1816–25", *Journal of Southeast Asian Studies* 34, no. 2 (June 2003): 200.
2. Ibid.
3. Campo, "Discourse without Discussion", p. 212.
4. Ibid., p. 211.
5. Ibid., pp. 211–12.
6. See, for example, F.L. Dunn and D.F. Dunn, "Maritime Adaptations and Exploitation of Marine Resources in Sundaic Southeast Asian Prehistory",

in *Prehistoric Indonesia*, edited by Pieter van de Velde (Dordrecht-Holland: Foris Publications, 1984), pp. 244–71; Richard A. Engelhardt and Pamela Rumball Rogers, "The Phuket Project Revisited: The Ethno-archaeology Through Time of Maritime Adapted Communities in Southeast Asia", *Journal of the Siam Society* 85 (1997): 17–33; C. Sather, "Sea Nomads and Rainforest Hunter-Gatherers: Foraging Adaptations in the Indo- Malaysian Archipelago", in *The Austronesians: Historical and Comparative Perspectives*, edited by P. Bellwood, J.J. Fo and D. Tryon (Canberra: Department of Anthropology, Research School of Pacific and Asian Studies, Australian National University, 1995), pp. 229–68.

7. Although still controversial and disputed, boats must have been in the region at least by the time of the first Austronesian migrations through maritime Southeast Asia, likely starting from Taiwan, approximately 3000 BCE (Peter Bellwood, *Prehistory of the Indo-Malayan Archipelago*, rev. ed. [Honolulu: University of Hawaii Press, 1997], p. 201). Some authors have suggested seafaring technology may have even predated the Austronesians by thousands of years in order to explain migrations from the Indonesian Archipelago to areas of eastern Indonesia and to Australia (Robert G. Bednarik, "An Experiment in Pleistocene Seafaring", *International Journal of Nautical Archaeology* 27, no. 2 [1998]: 139–49).

8. Jan Wisseman Christie, "State Formation in Early Maritime Southeast Asia: A Consideration of the Theories and the Data", *Bijdragen tot de Taal-, Land- en Volkenkunde* 151. no. 2 (1995): 246.

9. James Legge, *A Record of Buddhistic Kingdoms* (Oxford: Clarendon Press, 1886; unaltered reprint, New York: Paragon Book Reprint Corp., Dover Publications, Inc., 1965), p. 112; Paul Wheatley, *The Golden Khersonese* (Kuala Lumpur: University of Malay Press, 1961), p. 37.

10. Wheatley, *Golden Khersonese*, pp. 47, 57.

11. Personal communication, Pang Yong, 3 February 2004; Jeffery Hayes, 3 February 2004; and Koh Keng We, 4 February 2004 and 6 February 2004.

12. Wheatley, *Golden Khersonese*, p. 226.

13. Carl A. Trocki, *Prince of Pirates* (Singapore: Singapore University Press, 1979), p. 56.

14. See Barbara Andaya, "The Role of the Anak Raja", *Journal of Southeast Asian Studies* 7, no. 2 (1976); and Timothy Barnard, "Multiple Centers of Authority", (Ph.D. dissertation, University of Hawaii at Manoa, 1998).

15. Andi Zainal Abidin, *Sekali Lagi La Ma'dukelleng Arung Singkang* [Once Again La Ma'dukelleng Arung Singkang] (Ujung Pandang: Panitia Dasa Warsa IKIP, 1975), pp. 2, 9, 26.

16. William Henry Scott, *Barangay* (Manila: Ateneo De Manila University Press, 1999), pp. 154, 156–57.

17. See Defoe's early eighteenth century classic *A General History of the Robberies and Murders of the Most Notorious Pyrates*, for various descriptions of the

wretched forced to piracy or those that openly chose the path. See as well
C. Whitehead Esq., *Lives and Exploits of English Highwaymen, Pirates and
Robbers* (London: Charles Daly, 19, Red Lion Square, Holborn, 1839) for
similar descriptions of pirates.

18. See the 1959 Wilkinson Malay/English Dictionary, p. 655 for a definition of
    Illanun, or *Lanun*, and see Ali Haji ibn Ahmad, *The Precious Gift: Tuhfat al-
    Nafis*, translated by Virginia Matheson and Barbara Watson-Andaya (Kuala
    Lumpur: Oxford University Press, 1982), pp. 261–62, for a primary account
    of their raiding style.

19. See Nicholas Tarling, *Piracy and Politics in the Malay World* (Melbourne: F.W.
    Cheshire, 1963); and Trocki, *Prince of Pirates*, p. 1979, for a good account of
    the political developments of the late eighteenth and nineteenth century in
    the Malay world.

20. Tarling, *Piracy and Politics*, p. 1.

21. Barbara Watson-Andaya and Leonard Y. Andaya, *A History of Malaysia*, 2nd
    ed. (Honolulu: University of Hawaii Press, 2001), p 84.

22. See Abidin, *Sekali Lagi Ma'dukellong*, for a detailed account of the political
    intrigues and wars that were constantly fought between the kingdoms of
    southern Sulawesi against each other and the Dutch.

23. Leonard Andaya, *The Kingdom of Johor*, 1641–1728 (Kuala Lumpur: Oxford
    University Press, 1975), p. 120.

24. Andaya and Andaya, *History of Malaysia*, p. 83.

25. See Ahmad, *Precious Gift*, for an interesting account of Buginese rulers of
    Riau and detailed discussions of local and regional politcs from their
    perspective.

26. Dian Murray, *Pirates of the South China Coast 1790–1810* (Stanford: Stanford
    University Press, 1987), 24.

27. Ibid.

28. Ibid., p. 21.

29. Ibid., p. 40.

30. Ibid., p. 33.

31. Ibid., pp. 57, 71.

32. Ibid., p. 41.

33. Ibid., pp. 140–43.

34. For this discussion "Malay" includes a number of peoples all being loosely
    identified in the same socio-cultural-ethnic group historically, and in no
    way refers to the modern nation-state of Malaysia.

35. See, for example, in chronological order, J.C. van Leur, *Indonesian Trade and
    Society: Essays in Asian Social and Economic History* (Bandung: Sumur Bandung,
    1960); O.W. Wolters, *Early Indonesian Commerce* (Ithaca: Cornell University
    Press, 1967); D.G.E. Hall, A History of Southeast Asia (New York,
    St Martin's Press: 1968); O.W. Wolters, *The Fall of Srivijaya* (Ithaca: Cornell
    University Press, 1970); Kenneth R. Hall, *Maritime Trade and State*

Development in Early Southeast Asia (Honolulu: University of Hawaii Press, 1985); P.Y. Manguin, "City-States and City-State Culture in pre-15th Century Southeast Asia", in *A Comparative Study of Thirty City-State Cultures*, edited by M.H. Hansen, Historisk-filosofiske Skrifter 21 (Copenhagen: The Royal Danish Academy of Sciences and Letters), pp. 409–16; Christie, "State Formation", pp. 235–88.

36. O. W. Wolters, *History, Culture, and Region in Southeast Asian Perspectives*, Southeast Asia Program Publications, no. 26 revised (Ithaca: Cornell Southeast Asia Programs Publications, 1999), pp. 112–13.

37. Dianne Lewis, *Jan Compagnie in the Straits of Malacca, 1641–1795* (Athens, Ohio: Ohio University Center for International Studies, 1995), p. 9.

38. Ahmad, *Precious Gift*, pp. 193–94. Interestingly, Ahmad records that many people forcibly taken decided to stay voluntarily after a while, and eventually their families decided to come join them at their new homes.

39. The importance of prestige goods trade was not limited to the Malay orbit of power, but was also important historically in other parts of maritime Southeast Asia. See, for example, Laura Junker's work on prestige good trade in the Bais region of Negros, L. Junker, "Craft Good Specialization and Prestige Goods Exchange in Philippine Chiefdoms of the Fifteenth and Sixteenth Centuries", *Asian Perspectives* 32, no. 1 (1999): 1–36.

40. Wolters, *Fall of Srivijaya*, p. 93.

41. See Ahmad, *Precious Gift*, in which "piracies" of Orang Laut groups are a ubiquitous feature of this time, suggesting the fragmented political authority of the time.

42. Manguin, "City-States", p. 409.

43. Ahmad, *Precious Gift*, pp. 270–71.

44. Andaya, L., *Kingdom of Johor*, pp. 45–47.

45. Tarling, *Piracy and Politics*, p. 8; James Warren, *Iranun and Balangingi: Globalization, Maritime Raiding and the Birth of Ethnicity* (Quezon City: New Day Publishers 2002), pp. 20–22.

46. Benedict Sandin, *The Sea Dayaks of Borneo* (Michigan State University Press, 1967), p. 59.

47. Ibid., p. xv.

48. Ibid., pp. 66–67.

49. Ibid., pp. 63–64.

50. Ibid., p. xv.

51. Ibid., p. 60.

52. See Henry Keppel and James Brooke, *The Expedition of the H.M.S. Dido* (New York: Oxford University Press, 1991) for a full account of their recollections of these events.

53. Sandin, *Sea Dayaks*, p. 61.

54. Robert Pringle, *Rajahs and Rebels: The Ibans of Sarawak under Brooke Rule, 1841–1941* (Ithaca: Cornell University Press, 1970), p. 46.

55. Ulla Wagner, *Colonialism and Iban Warfare* (Stockholm: OBE-Tryck, 1972), pp. 141–42.

56. There is a short story related in several of the sources I consulted that explain why head-taking was necessary for marriage, part of a fertility ritual, and in many cases appears to have been a prerequisite of women before they would consent to the union. The story involves a man and a woman, and the man has just proposed to the woman. She refuses, and so the man goes to the forest and brings back a deer which he lays at her feet. She is not impressed, and so the young man goes back into the jungle and comes back with the head of an orangutan. Again, the woman is not impressed and so the man goes back into the jungle, and this time he returns with a human head which he lays at her feet. This time the woman takes due note and then agrees to marry the man. See Wagner, *Colonialism and Iban Warfare*, p. 132, and Edwin H. Gomes, *Seventeen Years Among the Sea Dyaks of Borneo* (Philadelphia: J.B. Lippincott Company, 1911), p. 74.

57. Wagner, *Colonialism and Iban Warfare* p. 142.

58. Ibid.

59. Gomes, *Seventeen Years*, p. 74.

60. The name "Iranun" refers to a specific ethnic group in the southern Philippines, but is also used to collectively refer to several groups, such as the Balangingi, Bajau, and Tausug, of predominantly Muslim raiders under the authority of the Sulu Sultanate. This discussion will use "Iranun" in the latter sense. This collective representation of southern Filipino raiders, despite its problematic generalizations, is adopted to facilitate and simplify analysis, and also because in much of Southeast Asia these raiders were often known by the collective representation of *Illanun, Lanun,* or *Iranun.*

61. Warren, *Iranun and Balangingi*, p. 38.

62. See ibid. and his other works: *The Sulu Zone* (Singapore: Singapore University Press, 1981); "Slave Markets and Exchange in the Malay World", *Journal of Southeast Asian Studies* 8, no. 2 (1977): 162–75; "Who Were the Balangingi Samal?", *Journal of Asian Studies* 37, no. 3 (1978): 477–90; and *The Global Economy and the Sulu Zone* (Quezon City: New Day Publishers, 2000).

63. Warren, *Iranun and Balangingi*, p. 26. The volcanic eruption pushing many Iranun to pursue raiding as a livelihood is anecdotally comparable to the economic crash in 1997, another act of God that stimulated piracy within an already established context.

64. Scott, *Barangay*, pp. 217–43.

65. Warren, *Iranun and Balangingi*, p. 167.

66. Ibid., p. 124; Ahmad, *Precious Gift*, pp. 261–64.

67. Warren, *Iranun and Balangingi*, p. 164.

68. Nicholas Tarling, *Southeast Asia: A Modern History* (Victoria: Oxford University Press, 2001), p. 263.

69. Warren, *Iranun and Balangingi*, 2002, pp. 167–68.
70. Ibid., p. 164.
71. Ibid., p. 209.
72. Ibid., pp. 173–74.
73. Ibid., p. 218.
74. Ibid., p. 101; Luis C. Dery, "Moro Raids and Their Impact on Luzon and the Visayas", paper presented at the 34th International Congress for Asian and Northern African Studies (ICANAS), University of Hong Kong, 1993, pp. 21–22, 27–30.
75. Dery, "Moro Raids", pp. 27–30.
76. Greg Bankoff, *Crime, Society, and the State in the Nineteenth Century Philippines* (Manila: Ateneo de Manila University Press, 1996), p. 191.
77. Warren, *Iranun and Balangingi*, p. 72.
78. Eric Tagliacozzo, *Secret Trades of the Straits: Smuggling and State-formation along a Southeast Asian Frontier, 1870–1910* (Hartford: Yale University Press, 1999), pp. 237–38.
79. Andaya and Andaya, *History of Malaysia*, p. 109.
80. Warren, *Iranun and Balangingi*, p. 64.
81. Campo, "Discourse without Discussion", p. 209.
82. A British ship of the line in the mid-nineteenth century could mount 100 plus cannon and carry 850 to 875 men (*Maritime History and Naval Heritage*, http://www.cronab.demon.co.uk/gen1.htm (accessed 27 March 2004), and even smaller warships such as frigates could mount 22 to 44 cannon (*Nationmaster.com*, http://www.nationmaster.com/encyclopedia/Frigate (accessed 27 March 2004), dwarfing native vessels like the *joanga*.
83. Campo, "Discourse without Discussion", p. 209.
84. Tagliacozzo, *Secret Trades*, p. 239, relates a story where a British warship had too deep a draught to approach the Borneo shore over the mudflats to pursue erstwhile "pirates", and so had to stand off at 900 yards and try to bombard them! This well demonstrates the technological advantages of the Europeans, being able to fairly accurately bombard targets half a mile distant, while also showing the advantages of local ship technology as well.
85. Leonard Andaya, "Interactions with the Outside World and Adaptation in Southeast Asian Society, 1500–1800", in *The Cambridge History of Southeast Asia*, Vol. 1, Part two, edited by Nicholas Tarling (Cambridge: Cambridge University Press, 1999), p. 41.
86. Ibid., p. 42.
87. Warren, *Iranun and Balangingi*, p. 191.
88. Tagliacozzo, *Secret Trades*, pp. 377–78, however, notes that arms traders in the late nineteenth and early twentieth centuries, despite colonial controls, still managed to smuggle arms. Smugglers used increasingly complex schemes of evasion and utilized the porous borders of the region, taking advantage of the frequent lack of co-operation between states.

89. Ibid., pp. 119-20.
90. Similarly, in modern times pirates have disabled navigation buoys to lure ships onto shoals, where they are then plundered ("Piracy Resurgence on the High Seas", *The Australian*, 8 November 1978, p. 11).
91. Tagliacozzo, *Secret Trades*, p. 120. See also the compendious volume N.F.M. a Campo, *Engines of Empire* (Hilversum, NL: Verloren, 2002), for an in-depth look at the role of steam power in expanding the Dutch empire in the East Indies.
92. Daniel R. Headrick, *The Tools of Empire* (New York: Oxford University Press, 1981), pp. 159-61.
93. Testimony of Nakhoda Mumin of Oya in "Reports of Brook Inquiry", *British Parliamentary Thesiss*, vol. 1854-55 (1976): 24, quoted in Robert Pringle, *Rajahs and Rebels: The Ibans of Sarawak under Brooke Rule, 1841-1941* (Ithaca: Cornell University Press, 1970), p. 48.
94. Warren, *Iranun and Balangingi*, p. 379.
95. Tagliacozzo, *Secret Trades*, p. 242.
96. Interestingly, although far outside the orbit of Southeast Asia, piracy/privateering in the Mediterranean carried out by the Barbary States from the seventeenth to the nineteenth centuries, and a variety of other small polities, including the old crusader order of the Knights of Malta, were similarly allowed to exist because of bickering between regional states. Despite repeated attacks on European and United States shipping in the late eighteenth and early nineteenth centuries, these nations could not put their own differences aside to deal with the Barbary States. In fact, similar to how the British sought to use Iranun raiders against the Dutch in the Moluccas, European, United States, and Middle East states would sign treaties (often observed more in the breach) with the corsairs whereby their ships could pass unharmed, leaving their rivals to bear the brunt of their predatory maritime activities (Cyrus H. Karakker, *Piracy was a Business* [Rindge, New Hampshire: R.R. Smith, 1953], pp. 32-33. In this way the Barbary States successfully operated in the Mediterranean from the seventeenth to the nineteenth century, 200 years or more!
97. Tarling, *Piracy and Politics*, pp. 14, 16, 20. Indeed the first twenty pages of the volume establish the supposition that the suppression of piracy was important in the expansion of British power in the Malay world in the nineteenth century, which the rest of the book then seeks to demonstrate.
98. Campo, "Discourse without Discussion", p. 209.
99. As may be seen from the Battle of *Beting Marau*, as one of the largest "anti-piracy" missions in the Malay world, where Brooke in command of a composite force of British warships and Iban *prahu*, decimated a rival contingent of Iban raiders, or "pirates" as Brooke saw them, did not happen until July of 1849 (Pringle, *Rajahs and Rebels*, p. 81). Likewise, Spanish attacks on the home bases of Iranun and Balangingi in the Sulu archipelago

were not carried out until the 1840s, and again in the 1860s, when steam ships made these attacks possible.

100. There is a lot of literature dealing with the idea of "criminal" activity and colonial state control, but not very much concerning the maritime realm. For example, see H.S. Nordholt, "The Jago in the Shadow: Crime and 'Order' in the Colonial State in Java", *Review of Indonesian and Malaysian Affairs* 25, no. 1 (1991): 74–91; who suggests that the Dutch really had very little control over most of Java, as exhibited by the extensive networks of *jagos*, local heroes/thugs. Bankoff describes a scene where accompanying rapid, uneven economic and population growth, there was a marked rise in criminality, in large part due to ineffective and/or limited Spanish control of the countryside (Bankoff, *Crime, Society and the State*, pp. 13–18). A similar theme is common through many of the works in: *Figures of Criminality in Indonesia, the Philippines, and Colonial Vietnam*, edited by V. L. Rafael (Ithaca, N.Y.: Southeast Asia Program Publications Southeast Asia Program Cornell University, 1999). While none of these directly deal with control of the maritime realm, they are analogous and suggestive of the limits of colonial influence on "criminal" activities in general.

101. Eric Tagliacozzo, "Kettle on a Slow Boil: Batavia's Threat Perceptions in the Indies Outer Islands, 1870–1910", *Journal of Southeast Asian Studies* 31, no. 1 (March 2000): 74.

3

Causative Factors of Contemporary Piracy

This chapter will explore causative factors of contemporary piracy through the lens of state control, exploring three aspects: (1) the marginalization of maritime peoples, (2) gaps in the political hegemony of states, and (3) tools, intelligence, tactics, and complimentary technology. The first section will examine the marginalization of maritime peoples, emphasizing economic conditions, access to and participation in national identities, and the role of a widespread maritime-oriented socio-cultural matrix. The second section will explore gaps in the political hegemony of regional states and why they have developed, which create space for piracy and other illicit activities that, in turn, further widen these gaps and stimulate an environment where piracy can grow. The third section will look at some of the operational details of piracy, discussing factors that allow them to operate effectively as well as factors affecting the state's ability to address piracy At the end of each section these factors will be compared with the causative factors of historical piracy detailed in Chapter 2. From this comparison a continuity of causative factors emerges suggesting how the roots of contemporary piracy may be addressed. The final section will be a summary of the causative factors and historical continuities and discontinuities of piracy.

MARGINALIZATION OF MARITIME-ORIENTED PEOPLE

There is a large segment of maritime-oriented peoples in Southeast Asia living a marginalized lifestyle, which collectively forms a large potential labour pool for piracy.[1] This marginalized group of maritime-oriented peoples not only forms a labour pool for piracy from which the majority of piracy stems, but it also constitutes the majority of victims as well. The first section will discuss the endemic poverty of many maritime-oriented peoples, and how uneven economic and weak political development over the last thirty years has done little to improve their conditions or draw them under state control. This theme will be further expanded upon in terms of the state's inability to provide many maritime peoples with a constructive role in the national identity. This situation will be examined further by drawing parallels between Hobsbawm's ideas on social banditry and piracy, as well as discussing the motivation inherent in the close proximity of "haves" and "have-nots". The final section will highlight and examine continuities and discontinuities between contemporary and historical causative factors of piracy, drawing on relevant historical context from Chapter 2.

Economic Development and Globalization

Over the last thirty years the processes of globalization have stimulated widespread economic growth throughout Southeast and East Asia, leading to a rapid pace of development. When measured in terms of gross domestic product (GDP) and the standard measures of industrial output, as well as standard markers of human conditions like literacy, infant mortality rates, and life expectancy, Southeast Asia has made impressive progress since the 1960s.[2] Despite post-modern debates about definitions of poverty, overall real strides have been made in reducing poverty, and generally increasing the material standard of life for people in many parts of Southeast Asia.[3] However, the rapid economic development of the last thirty years has been uneven, and has had unintended, negative consequences that are important for understanding why piracy has resurfaced as a significant threat in the region.

One of the primary problems is that political development in the region has not kept pace with economic development.[4] Despite unprecedented growth and the very real material gains that have been made, there are still large portions of populations that have either been left behind without access to economic opportunity, or have become unwitting victims of the rapid economic development, including many groups of maritime-oriented peoples. Historic social networks are breaking down as traditional economic and social systems give way and adapt to the pace of modernization.[5] Many regional governments are unwilling or unable to help those who are being left behind. Factories are attracting thousands of young people from villages to pursue more viable livelihoods and, while many continue to financially support their families, their absence is a missing link in the traditional social security network. This combined with an almost complete lack of institutionalized social security has left many facing new survival challenges.

The negative aspects of economic development and globalization have stimulated massive dislocation of populations, as millions of people move in search of better wages, even moving across international boundaries.[6] This development has provided opportunities for legitimate employment. However, it has also led to rising incidences of poverty, creating a labour pool for criminal activities like prostitution, drugs, petty extortion rackets, among many others, and when the right seafaring skills are available, possibly piracy. These problems which have manifested themselves during years of economic growth suggest weak state development, or simply economic development that has outpaced the capacity of the state to redistribute the profits effectively.

Economic growth in the region, especially East Asia, has translated into heavy increases in sea traffic through Southeast Asia, stimulating maritime economies but also creating new regulatory problems. As mentioned earlier more than 50,000 ships annually transit these waters, only inclusive of large freighters and tankers. Furthermore, total numbers of tonnage during 2004 were expected to rise 9.2 per cent, and twenty-foot container equivalents (TEUs) were expected to climb 6.8 per cent, largely due to the expanding Chinese economy,[7] with overall world trade expected to have risen 8.5 per cent despite rising oil prices,[8] which means increasing traffic through the pirate-infested waters of maritime Southeast Asia. Not only does this mean more ships to track, and a greater number of potential targets for pirates, but it also means that there will be more crews to try and track as well.

Seafarers numbering 1.2 million, or half the world merchant fleet, sail under flags of convenience, which means "ships can be owned by nationals of one country and be registered in another," and most "major ship-owning nations sail under flags of convenience", providing registration for boats and crews as a business.[9] Flags of convenience problematize the tracking of true identities of crew and ships, but they offer seafarers the opportunity to make wages far higher than under their own national flags. Therefore it is not in their interest to question ownership of the boat or the identities of the crew, and therefore screening processes are minimal. Lax enforcement of regulations is compounded by relatively easy access to forged documents, as pirates have been caught with passports from multiple countries, making their identification difficult.[10] In 2001 alone the International Maritime Organization (IMO) reported 13,000 cases of falsified documents among various ships crew, most of which were from Indonesia and the Philippines.[11] This provides easy opportunities for insiders to be planted who can relay boat position, crew compliment and/or ship layout to attackers.

Subsistence Economy

A significant portion of the total population of Southeast Asia lives near the coast and are dependent on the seas for their food and livelihoods.[12] For example, in 1998 in the Philippines approximately one million people were employed in fishing, or approximately 5 per cent of the work force, of which only 57,000 were employed on large vessels, implying the rest were small-scale fishermen.[13] In Indonesia at the same time there were approximately 4.6 million people employed in fishing, or approximately 4 per cent of the population if their families are included.[14] These figures represent only those reported to the government, and likely there are millions more people who earn some part of their living from the seas that do not report to the government, such as the Orang Laut and Bajau that will be discussed later in this chapter. These numbers also do not include the tens of thousands of small traders and merchants who ply these waters.

In both trades, even under ideal circumstances, individual operators without substantial personal capital are often at the margins of poverty, making enough to repay debt and provide the essentials of survival, but little else. Like their poor counterparts on land who have little money for capital improvements or to buy more land to farm, maritime peoples maintain a tenuous balance of sustainable survival,[15] especially as they often find themselves in some of the poorest regions of Southeast Asia, and isolated from major economic centres.[16]

Fishing catches can be fickle, depending on either unpredictable or uncontrollable variables like the weather, and fluctuations in the local and international markets can be potentially disastrous. In the contemporary world, fisher folk are also beset by massive illegal fishing operations (which many poor folks also engage in) that use dynamiting techniques or worse,[17] destroying reefs, fish habitat, and maritime people's future livelihood.[18] There is also massive illegal fishing in the form of unregistered foreign vessels who "pirate" the waters for increasingly rare fish. Rapid economic growth has severely damaged much of the environment on which many depend for their livelihoods, either through over-exploitation or pollution. As catches decline across the region competition for what is left increases. Facing these challenges, maritime peoples are generally the poorest of the poor, having to eke out a living from finicky resources that are frequently under attack, and the possibility of bringing home the equivalent of a year's income, or more, in one raid must prove an irresistible temptation to some.[19] For example, Thai fishermen who traditionally operated in the Gulf of Thailand began to seriously deplete fish stocks by the 1970s,[20] and moved out into other nations' waters, or were forced to find other sources of income, such as preying on Vietnamese boat people.[21] As one representative of a shipping company said, "Some of these ships can feed a whole Indonesian village. And these guys have nothing to lose."[22]

Economic Crises

The Asian economic crisis of 1997 exacerbated the problems that had developed during times of relative prosperity: the inequalities of rapid economic development, the resulting marginalization and dislocation of people, the expansion of organized criminal networks (discussed in more detail in the next section), over all aspects of weak state development, and the resurgence of piracy. Even though some authors have convincingly argued that Southeast Asians have weathered the economic crisis better than some of the direst predictions,[23] there was unarguably considerable affects, which stimulated piracy.

One of the most destructive aspects of the crisis was the rapidity with which it seized the region. The linked markets and interconnected economic structures forged through processes of globalization, and built upon questionable political and economic policy, created a monetary ripple in Thailand that quickly grew into a tsunami that inundated the region. Markets tumbled so quickly that responses were too slow in coming to stave off disaster for many states. Indonesia in particular was hard hit with massive unemployment, consumer price indices jumped to as high as 77 per cent, leading to high expenditures on daily necessities like food (up to 62 per cent of income in 1999), and approximately 18 per cent of people lived below the poverty line.[24] Many of these statistics have improved in the last couple of years, but between 1997 and 1999 the general welfare of Indonesian people as a result of the economic crisis was deeply affected. In the Philippines despite growing national income and savings levels, poverty and unemployment are also on the rise, particularly in those regions where piracy and smuggling have emerged as major problems, such as the southern Philippines and the Autonomous Region of Muslim Mindanao (ARMM), including Jolo and Tawi Tawi in the Sulu Sea.[25]

While the economic crisis was instrumental in the recent upsurge in piracy of the last five to six years, piracy numbers had begun to climb in the 1970s, 80s and 90s, starting in 1975 following the end of the Vietnam

Conflict, and continuing through the 1980s, with hundreds of attacks on Vietnamese refugees ("boat people") in the Gulf of Thailand and around Hong Kong, as well as a surge of incidents in the Sulu region.[26] These trends began during some of the biggest boom years in Southeast Asia. Uneven, rapid economic development without commensurate political development to control the expanding economies created the foundations of poverty, which in part stimulated the rise of piracy, and the economic crisis only made existing conditions worse.

A Stake in the National Identity

Maritime peoples often find themselves at the social and economic margins of societies that are terra firma-centric. In a modern nation-state, land is the primary focus of the state,[27] even if it is fragmented archipelagic islands. Modern states are physically defined by the territory they encompass, and until recently with developments regarding coastal waters and the Exclusive Economic Zone (EEZ),[28] this territory did not extend much beyond the coastline. In this way those who make their living from the seas are literally at the margins of state and society. The dominant political and social centres of most states are land-based agrarian societies, putting the maritime peoples' culture and society outside the dominant socio-cultural complex. This idea can be seen in the negative treatment of traditionally nomadic and semi-nomadic sea peoples whose tenure on land was very limited or non-existent.[29] These peoples existed almost entirely on the seas, and as such were only tied to landed political centres through patron–client ties where they provided some goods or service in return for protection. This marginal position has accorded them a low position in local social hierarchies.

The most extreme examples are those groups like the Orang Laut and Bajau Laut who traditionally spent the majority of their time on the seas, although in recent decades many of these groups have settled on land and are trying to avail themselves of the economic and educational opportunities there. The Bajau Laut in Sabah, Malaysia, part of a group spanning the Sulu Archipelago, are one case in point. In these waters the dominant social and political group are the Tausug, a land-based, agricultural, Islamic ethnic group. In this situation the Bajau came to occupy the very bottom of the social-political hierarchy, because they were primarily sea-based, considered without roots or property, and were largely animist. These traditional systems have changed as the patron–client ties that bound the Bajau and Tausug have eroded since the introduction of a monetary trading system in the late nineteenth and early twentieth centuries.[30] However, only in the 1950s and 60s did many Bajau settle on land and convert to Islam. These divisions still persist, however, especially since the arrival of thousands of Filipino Bajau in the 1970s and 80s.[31] As newcomers they have been frequently relegated to more menial jobs and forced to live on their boats due to their financial situation. Furthermore, they are obliged to engage in patron–client relationships to maintain their visa statuses and enter the established social and political networks, where they are filling the lower ranks of society.

Similarly, the Orang Laut[32] while once the backbone of power in the Strait of Malacca region dominated by Malay maritime states, they have faded into the background. This process started with the rise of the Bugis in the Malay world during the eighteenth century, and the marginalization of previous power structures that had been based on the incorporation of the Orang Laut. The process continued as these maritime states became landed bureaucracies under expanding English control in the nineteenth century,[33] under which the Orang Laut never re-established their pre-eminence. Even today many of the Orang Laut remain outside the mainstream of national development, as their lifestyle has become increasingly at odds with ideas of national identity and economic progress.[34]

Additionally, in the past the loyalty of maritime peoples, like the Orang Laut, could be commanded by the personal charisma and spiritual potency of their immediate leaders through the chain of hierarchies, eventually to the ruler. The amorphous modern state is not able to effectively step into this role, as power and authority are frequently far removed physically in the national capital, and conceptually as maritime peoples have little to do with the power structure by which they are now governed. Furthermore, beyond the lack of representation or political power, these people have been left behind in the rapidly developing economy. Sometimes this is by choice as they do not see what they can gain from the state, but it is also a failure to successfully draw them into the economy. Contemporary states have failed to offer any attractive economic opportunity to these people and thus give them a stake in the goals and identity of the state. Not being able to command the personal loyalties of these people has left them largely outside the state structure, despite technically existing within the claimed territory of such a state, and thus left to their own devices to make ends meet.

The state needs to be able to offer maritime peoples economic and social opportunities, and moreover "a more fundamental need is for the people ... to be treated as valued participants in the nation building process."[35] In the past socio-cultural links between the Orang Laut and the state could supersede to some degree the cyclic emergence of piracy. However, the development of new political and economic systems in the eighteenth and nineteenth century made Orang Laut navigational and seafaring skills, as well as their abilities as warriors, obsolete, and contemporary nation-states have yet to find a mutually suitable, constructive place for them in their structure. This is not to suggest that the Orang Laut per se are the hub of piracy in the modern world, but it does suggest that some maritime peoples have had difficulty aligning their "marginal" existence with contemporary states.

Labour Pool for Piracy

The social and economic marginalization of maritime peoples, in large part arising from poor state control and/or regulation of the economy, and the inability to effectively include maritime peoples in the national identity, has created a large potential labour pool for piracy, some of whom have become agents of piracy. Despite the presence of states that ostensibly had control over these vast seascapes, there was never a time when raiding/piracy had been entirely suppressed, and there has been a continual occurrence of piracy until the present day.[36] However, it has only been in the last thirty years, and particularly in the last twelve to fifteen years, that piracy has resurfaced sufficiently to garner the steady attention of analysts and the media. The continuous presence of piracy in the region, the potential cultural continuities preserving some element of raiding cultures from the past, and as incidences of contemporary piracy are geographically contiguous with hotspots of historical raiding, suggests connections between contemporary acts of piracy and its historical counterparts. Inter-village raids and frequent attacks on fishing vessels during times of poor catches reported during the 1950s and 60s,[37] as well as attacks on Vietnamese boat people in the 1970s and 80s, and incidents in the Sulu Sea around the same time, suggests that in times of economic hardship piracy is still a viable option for some maritime peoples. As Vagg suggests, their traditions may present piracy as a viable, "culturally 'thinkable'" option.[38]

The seas provide a literal and metaphorical underlying continuity that link maritime peoples in divergent places providing a physical constant around which they organize their lives. This orientation provides some of the essential requirements for any would-be pirate, such as nautical skills, local knowledge of seas and geography, and quite simply the willingness to commit theft on sea rather than on land. For these reasons maritime peoples are a large potential labour pool for piracy. This labour pool can be broadly characterized as having seafaring and nautical skills, being poor, socio-economically marginalized, and potentially come from a cultural matrix where piracy is "thinkable". This sketch is not remarkable for its accuracy in describing would-be pirates, but rather is remarkable because it points to such a large segment of maritime Southeast Asia that may have sufficient motivation to be considered potential pirates.

In a bitter irony, the majority of piracy — low-end ad hoc organization — is emerging from this marginalized labour pool, and the majority of their victims are also from this group. The "easy" targets, such as fisher folk and local traders, often bear the brunt of attacks at sea, rather than the more highly publicized international shipping victims.[39] In a recent article, fishermen in northern Sumatra relate that they "tak berani melaut menyusul perompakan..." (are afraid to go to sea because of piracy).[40] Another article states that "almost two-thirds of the 12,000 fishing boats in Northern Sumatra were not operating because of piracy concerns."[41] Maritime peoples live in a dangerous world where pirates prey on whomever is around them. This situation is analogous to historical piracy where the majority of victims were also local traders and fisherman, while better defended European vessels were far less frequently molested.[42] Contemporarily it may not be that larger international vessels are better defended, but attacking them generally requires more organization and involves more risk, beyond what low-end pirates are regularly willing to tackle.

Social Piracy

The parallels between some aspects of low-end piracy, noted by Carolin Liss among others,[43] mirrors Hobsbawm's treatment of social banditry. Hobsbawm's social bandits are not seen as simple criminals in public opinion, rather they are heroes to the people, distinct from organized crime as well as distinct from traditional peoples for who raiding was a way of life.[44] According to Hobsbawm these social bandits "lie between the evolutionary phase of tribal and kinship organization, and modern capitalist and industrial society, but including phases of disintegrating kinship society and the transition to agrarian capitalism".[45] The subsistence needs and marginal lifestyle that drives much of low-end piracy is indeed in many ways distinct from the motivations of high-end piracy. Organized crime engages in risky attacks with expected returns far beyond that of survival needs, while low-end piracy has more modest goals and so engages in less risky attacks. The in-between "kinship organization, and modern capitalist and industrial society" also fits with what has been discussed above. Large segments of the maritime population have not been effectively incorporated into the state, either by colonial or the independent states, and as such remain isolated from the rapid economic development of the last thirty years. This could also be seen as characteristic of the "in-between" nature of social banditry, or social piracy. The "in-between" nature of social banditry fits various aspects of contemporary piracy, suggesting that criminal activity, potentially including piracy, results from poor economic and political development, and lack of incorporation into the dominant political structure.

In this situation it is conceivable that with chronic poverty as a backdrop, for the good of one's family or village, theft could be morally rationalized and even ethically justified. To offset a bad fishing season or to simply make ends meet some maritime peoples may turn to piracy. There are several accounts mirroring this line of logic, but it is unclear how pervasive this logic may be, or how "noble" these pirates really are.[46] If these acts are actually carried out for the good of the community or one's family is debatable, as it is not uncommon for pirates to pay off local villagers for their co-operation,[47] and how much of those profits trickle down to the villagers from the headmen is unknown.

This rationalization can be carried further if the victims appear to have far more money or goods than they need, essentially a situation of have and have-nots in close proximity. In this way, a passing foreign yacht would seem a justifiable target, just as would passing foreign freighters carrying goods and monies far beyond the normal reach of the would-be pirate through legal means, for example, poor villagers in Batam, Indonesia, looking across at the wealthy skyline of Singapore.[48] This rationalization could also be made more potent by moral judgements against the targets, identifying them not simply as justifiable targets, but as deserving to be stolen from. For instance, in describing acts of banditry against the Spanish in nineteenth century Philippines, Bankoff cites a common conception of the time "It is not a sin to rob a Spaniard."[49] In that situation the Spanish were held as a morally repugnant, an oppressive force that justified stealing from them. A similar attitude could be hypothesized in contemporary maritime Southeast Asia. Everyday ships laden with the bounty of foreign countries bound for the wealthy lands of other foreign countries pass by these marginalized, poor maritime peoples — the same waters from which maritime peoples try to eke out a meagre living, their "territory". Moreover this wealth passing through their territory without any repayment or compensation may even be goods produced in their own countries. Is it right that they should suffer from poverty when these wealthy foreigners extract goods and resources from their poor country, using their seas without contributing anything back?

The parallels with Hobsbawm's social banditry, and the justifications of the "have" and "have-nots", and "it is not a sin to rob a Spaniard", are limited however. Hobsbawm writes that social banditry cannot exist in a modern industrial society, yet many pirates use motorboats and modern technology that is only available in an industrialized world, and the majority of piracy victims are not castable as the rich foreign exploiter, but rather local fishermen. However, the "have" and "have-nots" perception could also be applied to local gaps between capital owners and labourers, or other "have-nots". While not as graphic as the gap between Singapore and Batam, or a foreign yacht and a local *prahu*, the gap is much closer to their everyday experiences. Furthermore, Hobsbawm's bandits are located outside the community, whereas historically piracy was a communal activity.[50] What they both suggest is a group of people isolated or disenfranchised from participating in the national economy and identity. From this position it is not difficult to establish a justification for piracy.

Causative Factors: Historical Continuities and Discontinuities

Maritime peoples in Southeast Asia are part of a socio-cultural matrix that exhibits links and continuities with the past. Ironically, maritime peoples comprise a large potential labour pool for piracy, and are also the largest group of victims of piracy. This matrix is characterized by a maritime orientation on the margins of the land, and consequently on the margins of land-oriented states, which has left many maritime peoples in the bottom rungs of the social, as well as, economic hierarchy. A key part of this maritime orientation is the practice of a broad-based survival strategy, maintaining fluidity and flexibility, to be able to switch from one resource to another and to take advantage when opportunity presents itself. This could mean fishing and aquaculture, catching

aquarium fish, collecting shells to sell, carrying trade goods on your boat
from one market to the next, carrying tourists around, producing crafts,
smuggling goods, or even piracy, just as raider groups of old could
seamlessly switch between raiding, trading and fishing, taking advantage
of whatever bounty the sea brought their way, including wayward
vessels. Contemporary maritime peoples likely exhibit similar fluidity in
their economic pursuits, fishing part-time, trading, maybe even being a
labourer, of which piracy forms a logical, justifiable, and "culturally
thinkable" option, even if only part-time both in percent of year or
labour time, but also in terms of total duration. Piracy could just be a
temporary job for a few years. As Dian Murray notes about fisher folk
off the coast of China and Vietnam in the early nineteenth century: "the
result was a livelihood [fishing] so miserable that, for many, a successful
piratical foray was the sole hope for a better life ... piracy as a temporary
survival strategy made sense."[51]

In order to control this potential labour pool for piracy, states need
to be able to successfully incorporate these people into the state. In the
past a combination of economic opportunity and personal loyalty held
many maritime peoples within the state. Modern states have not been
able to offer economic opportunity to large portions of these people, as
suggested by the prevalence of poverty. Moreover, the state has not
been able to fill the role of personal, charismatic leadership effective in
the past for incorporating maritime peoples or offer them a constructive
role in nation building. This has left maritime peoples on their own to
create their own opportunities and make ends meet, thus creating a
large potential labour pool for piracy. These conditions then respond to
broader economic and political circumstances, as was the case with
piracy in southern China in response to the Tay-son rebellion. The
economic crisis of the late 1990s was just such a stimulus and helped
create an increase in piracy.

Low-end ad hoc organized piracy and social piracy, characterized by
opportunistic and at times an apparently necessity-driven nature, both
reflect this marginal status of maritime peoples. Low-end piracy makes
up the majority of incidents, of which the majority of victims are likely
easy targets such as local fisher folk and traders. The idea of social
piracy suggests further potential links between marginalization and
justification for acts of piracy, linking the "in-between" status of maritime-
oriented peoples and weak structural development. Social piracy also
calls to mind historic conceptions of piracy as part of a respected socio-
economic system that was often community-based, suggesting direct

cultural links between some aspects of contemporary piracy and its historic counterparts.

The links between piracy and socio-cultural-economic marginality suggest a policy approach that focuses on incorporating maritime peoples into the economic and social identity of the state. While the state may not ever be capable of filling traditional leadership roles based on personal, charismatic prowess, it can extend economic opportunities to these people and positively include them in the national identity, and thus try to encourage their participation in legitimate economic activities of the state, countering the unavoidable cyclic economic and political processes that encourage piracy.

GAPS IN POLITICAL HEGEMONY

Piracy is a constant presence in the waters of Southeast Asia, lurking in the "sinews" of the state. It emerges from gaps in a state's political hegemony, where it is often only one of several challenges to political control, and further widens the gaps from which it emerged. It also enlarges the space for other illicit activities,[52] becoming an indicator of weak political control. While piracy does not directly threaten the collapse of any state in Southeast Asia today, it is a resurgence of non-state actors vying for "a piece of the pie" in a system where the legitimacy of the state largely depends on its ability to monopolize the means of violence, or at least its threat, within set territorial borders.[53] In claiming a monopoly on violence the state must also take responsibility for the violence that erupts and emanates from the state, and failure to do so is to weaken its claim to legitimacy. While the modern state has made more ambitious claims of control, the principle is similar as in the past. Piracy's virulent existence points to gaps in the state's political hegemony that allow it to thrive, questioning political authority and thereby challenging state claims of legitimacy.

This section will first explore several gaps in the political hegemony of regional states, focusing on Indonesia. First the physical and cultural geography of the region will be discussed and the particular challenges it poses in enforcing maritime boundaries. Then two examples of maritime crime will be examined — smuggling, and secessionist movements in Mindanao and Aceh, which both drain security resources, and help provide an environment where piracy can exist. It will then look at the patronage of piracy, examining how the widespread system of patron–client relations, particularly in connection with organized crime and corruption within the state, facilitate piracy. The later part of this section will discuss the problematic nature of international, multi-lateral co-operation in addressing piracy in recent years; as well as how this interacts with the low priority piracy receives on the domestic agenda of regional states like Indonesia. The section concludes with a summary and analysis drawing in historical context and relativizing these issues to security policy.

Physical and Cultural Geography

Natural boundaries in maritime Southeast Asia are virtually non-existent. The geography of maritime Southeast Asia defies the notion of static, territorially based boundaries, because the geography is so fluid. It was only in the nineteenth and twentieth centuries that nationalist powers conceived of demarcating and dividing these sea spaces in Southeast Asia, as previously it had not been of much concern. Both historically and presently the geography is incredibly complex, characterized by extensive coastlines, mazes of littoral mangrove and lowland swamps cut by riverine estuaries, spotted with sand banks and shifting waterways, and thousands of islands surrounded by innumerable reefs. Whereas the seas act as highways for trade and exchange, the interiors of islands are often divisive, being mountainous, frequently cut by unnavigable river valleys and ravines, covered in dense tropical jungle in the hills, and covered in swamps lower down, making overland networks difficult, and at times, impossible to maintain. Even contemporary overland transit is frequently not possible, as between islands, and is not as efficient as moving by sea.

The long and porous maritime borders established in the nineteenth century by colonial powers are still enforced by the littoral nations of the region. These borders have actually expanded with modern developments of Law of the Sea concerning territorial waters, archipelagic waters, and the EEZ, bringing that much more maritime territory ostensibly under state control.[54] Indonesia alone claims 81,000 km of coastline, 3 million square km of territorial waters, and an additional 3.1 million square km in their EEZ.[55] The Philippines has approximately 17,500 km of coastline, with a total maritime area (internal waters, territorial waters, EEZ) of 2,200,000 square km.[56]

For centuries maritime peoples had navigated the waters of Southeast Asia, fishing, trading, harvesting sea products, and raiding, with scant regard for imaginary boundaries, and they continued to do so despite what map makers in Europe had decided. Their lives and their cultures mimic the sea in some aspects, for just as the sea does not know borders, so the people who ply them have little respect for borders as well. Over the last thirty years there have been large population movements across international maritime borders that regional states have been unable to stop or control. During the 1970s, civil unrest and armed conflict in the southern Philippines caused thousands of Filipinos to migrate into Malaysia seeking safety and opportunity. Many of whom were Bajau, maritime peoples with historic connections to the areas around northern Malaysia and the southern Philippines. By 1979 "40 per cent of all Bajau Laut and 77 per cent of all other residents in the village [Bangau-Bangau]" were classified as *pelarian* or refugees, without Malaysian citizenship, and approximately 30,000 refugees had migrated from the southern Philippines to Sabah.[57] In some ways these migrations and labels of citizenship are rather arbitrary, considering that the Bajau Laut had roamed between the southern Philippines and Sabah long before national borders were drawn and citizenships had to be chosen.[58] Movement of people between Indonesia and Malaysia is likewise a persistent problem, as economic and cultural connections between the sides of the Strait of Malacca predate international boundaries. This movement has especially been of concern in recent years as the monetary crisis of 1997 hit Indonesia particularly hard, causing many Indonesians to seek their fortunes abroad.

Starting in 1975, and continuing for twenty-five years, an estimated 840,000 Vietnamese political and economic refugees, many of whom were "boat people", fled their country.[59] Hong Kong and other regional governments were forced to address the problem and bear much of the financial and political costs, albeit quite reluctantly in some cases, and many of these people were eventually repatriated, or relocated to the United States and Europe. The mass exodus well reflects the difficulties of maintaining borders in the maritime world, as one cannot put up walls to keep people out. Even in 1996, as an example of the difficulties these countries face, a newspaper article relates that Indonesia caught 10,096 ships docking illegally.[60]

Maritime Crime

It may seem odd to lump secessionist movements with smuggling. However, they are both examples of criminal activities (as viewed from the state) that are linked to the idea or act of piracy. Moreover, while these crimes do not fall within the working definition of piracy established for this text, they do create gaps in the state's political hegemony where piracy can operate and/or benefit from the gaps created by piracy.

Smuggling is ubiquitous in maritime Southeast Asia, particularly between Indonesia and Malaysia, just across the narrow Strait, and between Sabah, Malaysia, and the southern Philippines through the Sulu Archipelago. An indication as to the importance and pervasiveness of smuggling, during the Indonesian struggle for independence from the Dutch between 1945 and 1949 the Indonesian military was in dire financial problems, just like the rest of the country, and the military was forced to seek funding any way they could. This included smuggling rings that "although arising originally out of necessity, opened up opportunities for individuals to benefit personally."[61] The size of these smuggling operations started to dig into state coffers, however, and in 1967 the state tried to put a stop to these activities.[62] Furthermore, between Sumatra, Penang, and Singapore (among other ports in the Strait) during the Indonesian struggle against the Dutch, "huge quantities of goods were being shifted along the trade networks ... Hundreds of boats ... were working, making a mockery of Dutch attempts to impose a navel blockade on the Malacca Straits."[63] This was a concerted effort on the part of an organized movement, but it well illustrates the difficulties of preventing profitable, large-scale smuggling operations even using naval forces.

In the southern Philippines in more recent decades a gun-toting "wild west" atmosphere has emerged, where smugglers are armed to the teeth, and if they are not armed, such as hard-up fisher folk part-timing as local smugglers, they often fall prey to pirates who know that it is difficult to report stolen or smuggled goods.[64] The problem in recent years has reached the level where President Arroyo specifically mentioned the issue of smuggling when planning a national agenda.[65] Similarly, contemporarily in the Strait of Malacca smugglers bring cheap goods, timber, and even people,[66] from Indonesia to Malaysia, which has also received national and regional attention.[67] More than timber, cigarettes, or even people though, arms smuggling across these borders is of particular importance, just as it was in colonial times, because Indonesia and the Philippines face separatist movements in Aceh and Mindanao respectively. Light arms are easily transportable and therefore relatively easy to smuggle, thus making them available to any non-state actor with the necessary funds, including would-be pirates. Smuggling not only potentially provides pirates with weapons and materials, but also creates avenues by which their "booty" can be disposed of as well. The black markets found throughout maritime Southeast Asia rely on cheap goods, and they do not ask questions about their origins, whether smuggled or pirated (in this case both maritime piracy and electronic piracy).

Much of the arms smuggling in the Strait of Malacca stems from the Gerakan Aceh Merdeka (GAM, or the Free Aceh Movement), a militant secessionist movement based in northern Aceh province of Indonesia, whose goal is the formation of an independent Islamic state. This movement for independence has been ongoing since its start in 1976, as distinguished from the Darul Islam (Abode of Islam) uprising in the 1950s when Aceh sought economic and political autonomy within Indonesia, and not specifically national independence, as is the case now.[68] GAM's involvement in maritime crime is suggested by accusations of repeated acts of piracy (despite their avowed political motivations), including kidnappings, hijackings, and robberies, in order to raise funds for their operations. While these crimes do not fall under our rubric of piracy they are a serious gap in the political hegemony of Indonesia.

One kidnap victim on the Strait of Malacca reported that he was taken to a jungle base in Aceh, and that his captors spoke Acehnese.[69] Furthermore, the organization, weapons, clothes, and hair cuts, noticed in several attacks were suggestive of military personnel. Despite these allegations, GAM steadfastly denies any involvement in such operations, and there is no hard evidence linking them to these attacks.[70] Whether involved in piracy or not, GAM has carved out an area in Indonesia where state control does not extend, and GAM's control of the area is uncertain. In this area, with or without GAM's knowing, pirates are likely operating independently and taking advantage of the chaos in the region, and even mimicking GAM forces to misplace suspicion. Noel Choong, the head of the IMB Piracy Reporting Centre in Kuala Lumpur, recently stated in reference to kidnappings off Aceh's east coast that, "In the beginning, about five years ago, it was GAM. But in 2003, there were signs that it wasn't GAM doing it but organized criminal gangs. These are kidnap-for-profit operations, not separatists."[71]

GAM's activities while not piracy do have an impact on the general security of the region which in turn likely affects non-political acts of piracy. Additionally, GAM does have maritime capabilities, largely recruited from local sympathetic maritime peoples or possibly criminal networks. A smuggling network, particularly with connections to Penang, Malaysia where a substantial population of expatriate Acehnese live and there are Malaysians sympathetic to GAM's political and religious struggle,[72] through which arms, supplies, possibly recruits, and money are smuggled into Aceh. In order to shut down these networks and set up a blockade, the Indonesian military has sent most of their meagre operational naval capacity to Aceh, thus drawing it away from all other possible activities, such as anti-piracy patrols.

On the other side of maritime Southeast Asia, a similar situation to Aceh exists in the southern Philippines, in parts of Mindanao and the ARMM, established in 1987. Since the 1970s a number of militant Islamic groups have taken up arms to demand greater equality and/or independence from the Christian majority central government. Three major groups have emerged over the decades, the Moro National Liberation Front (MNLF), MILF, and Abu Sayyaf. The MNLF signed a peace treaty with the central government in 1996, officially ending their struggle. However, MILF, Abu Sayyaf, and various "lost commands" continue their armed struggle.[73] Accusations of piracy have been levelled at both MILF and Abu Sayyaf for recurrent spates of maritime violence, notably kidnapping tourists from the island of Sipadan in Malaysia,[74] and the Sasa Wharf bombing in Davao.[75] However, as violent or reprehensible as these maritime crimes are they also do not fit this book's working definition of piracy, as these groups have avowed political ambitions, for which they are engaging in militant acts and just happen to be using boats as a vehicle. MILF and Abu Sayyaf, however, like GAM, both have modest maritime capabilities, which form a network for smuggling through which they can acquire arms and other goods. Regardless of the merits of their struggle MILF and Abu Sayyaf have, like GAM, created an area where state control does not extend. These insurrections absorb military and police attention preventing them from deploying their resources elsewhere, and have created a wild west atmosphere in the southern Philippines where guns rule the waves.

Patronage of Piracy

Patronage of piracy provides important organizational and material support for piracy. It is important to note that patrons are not entirely necessary for most low-end ad hoc piracy, which makes up the majority of incidents. However this support appears to be a critical in the development of high-end organized piracy. As with the general description of maritime peoples in the previous chapter, this discussion is not particularly remarkable for being able to dissect the inner workings of piracy, but rather it is remarkable because it describes an existing, widespread system into which piracy can easily be accommodated.

Patron–client ties exist throughout the world, and in all times, where enhancing one's position is achieved through personal relationships rather than through a formalized system of "blind" meritocracy. What Aung-Thwin writes about Burma in the 1990s holds for much of Southeast Asia: "Patron-clientilism is still dominant at all levels and categories of society; authority and power are still intrinsic and not extrinsic ... loyalty is given more to the person than to an idea ..."[76] The "man of prowess", charismatic leadership, characteristic of historical political structures in maritime Southeast Asia, largely disappeared in any formalized context, but appears to remain embedded in the essence of patron–client relationships. Personal relationships are more important than the structured bureaucracy of business or government, and those who help you often expect something in return for that help. This *quid pro quo* arrangement, while highly simplified in concept, can become quite complex in arrangement. This fundamentally simple, yet highly flexible system allows groups to easily navigate between the various political systems and cultures of the region. This system forms the bedrock of personal and professional relations in many areas of Southeast Asia, incorporating disparate elements without having to create new power structures.

These relationships run the gamut from being called Asian values in some circumstances, to corruption and nepotism in other circumstances. The nature of these relationships allows for far greater personal influence on a system, so that they can function more efficiently and more judiciously than a "pure" meritocracy if headed by a strong, conscientious, personality, but can descend into blatant corruption in different circumstances. These systems create spaces where personal influence has untoward effects, ideal for a "behind the scenes" world of fluid and dynamic power structures, which piracy can take advantage of.

Organized Crime

Organized crime, like the term piracy itself, escapes easy definition, but for the sake of this discussion it will be understood as criminal activity that falls under the control of known criminal gangs, such as the triads or yakuza, or criminal activities that require large-scale organization.

Organized crime has made its presence felt throughout the region, from Hong Kong, Indonesia, Taiwan, the Philippines, Burma, Thailand, Laos, and stretching throughout East Asia as well.[77] Rapid economic development in the region has provided organized crime opportunity to expand their organizations, taking advantage of all the loose capital floating around. In hijacking/phantom ship cases such as the *Alondra Rainbow*,[78] *Petro Ranger*,[79] and *Tenyu*,[80] where the entire ship and cargo was taken, it is obvious that some sort of highly organized criminal gang was involved. Phantom ship incidents like these had become more common over the last few years, with sixteen hijackings reported worldwide in 2001 (double the number in 1999), and twenty-five in 2002.[81] However, numbers appear to be down for 2003 and 2004 despite a record high of reported piracy incidents in 2003.[82] A number of small boats, like tugs and barges, which could be used by syndicates in their smuggling operations, were reported lost, however.[83] One explanation for this pattern of high-end attacks is that organized crime was also affected by the 1997 monetary crisis, forcing them to diversify their operations, and thus the increase in high-end piracy.[84] Not all piracy is involved with organized crime, but when these operations have access to firearms, speed boats, shipping vessels, docking facilities, illegal markets, networks of informants, people in authority, and manpower, it increases the capabilities and ambitions of the pirates, posing a much greater challenge to political control.

Corruption and Governmental Complicity

Along with non-state actors, corrupt elements of states, including security forces, create security gaps and drain resources, important in considering the resurgence of piracy. Corruption is a widespread phenomenon throughout Southeast Asia, often taking advantage of the patron–client networks mentioned above, and is frequently the norm rather than the exception. China, Thailand, Vietnam, the Philippines, Malaysia, Burma, and Indonesia, all the littoral states in maritime Southeast Asia, with the *possible* exception of Singapore and its zero-tolerance policy, have their problems with corruption. In terms of piracy, corruption of state security forces is almost a prerequisite, especially for any operations larger than those involving local thugs.[85] As mentioned earlier pirates need certain things to be able to function, and two of those are a safe haven and markets for their stolen goods. Pirates do not exist as self-sufficient sea roamers who never touch land. They need the co-operation, or at least wilful ignorance of, a variety of land-based officials, such as harbour masters, village-level bureaucrats, and at least a few local police. The higher up corruption and connections extend, the more efficient and extensive the operation. A detailed study of the nature and extent of corruption from top to bottom in all these states is far beyond the scope of this book, but two examples will be looked at where they affect piracy more directly.

In the early and mid-1990s there were several reports connecting China with incidents of piracy in the South China Sea.[86] In 1991 and 1992 Chinese officials were accused of piracy for seizing a number of Vietnamese boats on charges of smuggling,[87] but more serious circumstances also developed. There were reports of official-looking uniformed personnel in patrol craft with Chinese markings and flying a red flag, which attacked several ships outside Chinese territorial waters. Additionally, several vessels accused of smuggling had been taken to southern Chinese ports by "customs officials", where they were asked for $500,000 for the return of their ship. When the money was not forthcoming the cargo was seized. Several high-publicity hijacking/piracy incidents, such as the *Tenyu*, the *Anna Sierra*, and the *Petro Ranger*, all involved Chinese officials, as the vessels were eventually recovered in Chinese waters. Ironically, two suspected Indonesian pirates from the *Anna Sierra* who had been released by Chinese officials, turned up in connection with the *Tenyu* case.[88] No hard evidence surfaced publicly linking Chinese officials and piracy, but it was readily apparent that Chinese ports, easily accessible from other pirate-prone areas such as the Strait of Malacca and the Hainan/Luzon/Hong Kong triangle, were operational safe havens for dealing with hijacked vessels. Following these events China was seen to crack down on piracy when thirty-eight arrests were made in connection with another hijacking. This was a particularly brutal case where the crew were bludgeoned to death and thrown overboard by pirates reportedly posing as Chinese customs officials.[89] Of the thirty-eight arrested, thirteen pirates, drunk on rice wine and chanting Ricky Martin's World Cup 1998 theme song, ironically titled "The Cup of Life", were executed.[90] Aside from possible corruption and the involvement of "rogue" Chinese officials, there was also speculation that some of these attacks may have been part of a broader Chinese policy aimed at extending their sovereignty in the South China Sea.[91] Chinese officials have denied any involvement, and following the arrests and executions noise seems to have died down concerning Chinese complicity in acts of piracy.

The Tentara Nasional Indonesia Angkatan Laut (TNI AL, or the Indonesian National Military Naval Forces),[92] like Chinese officials, has been implicated in acts of piracy, and/or in simply looking the other direction while it occurs,[93] but there is no concrete information linking the TNI AL to acts of piracy. However, there are a significant number of second-hand accounts, related interviews, and circumstantial evidence that implicates the Indonesian military at some level. Additionally, there is a history of extra-governmental funding and extra-legal activities suggesting that elements of the TNI in general may be open to involvement in "non-state" activities like piracy.

Interestingly even as late as 1980 the Indonesian military was responsible for funding up to 50 per cent of its own budget.[94] Currently the TNI still funds many of its operations through "offline incomes", meaning non-government appointed funds, from private business ventures and the like. The exact sources and quantity of these funds is not generally known and "even up to the highest level of the TNI there exists a genuine vagueness about how much the military earns from its businesses and what it is used for."[95] Additionally, in the wake of the Asian economic crisis funding for the Indonesian Navy was cut drastically. Moreover, the military's offline sources of income are planned to be taken over by the government in 2005, and it is unclear if the military received the larger budget it has requested.[96] The TNI's funding being rather opaque, and with major connections to private business and politics in a notably corrupt government,[97] suggests some amount of corruption within the ranks of the TNI. As mentioned above, the TNI has also been directly involved in smuggling operations. Although none of this is direct evidence for piracy, it does suggest willingness to, and a history of, engaging in extra-legal activities.

Specific allegations of TNI involvement in piracy are as murky as their budgetary situation, and consist mostly of hearsay and personal accounts, but they do cast long shadows of suspicion. One victim of a pirate raid was Captain Peter Newton of the British Navy, who was part of a group that helped train anti-piracy units in Indonesia. Captain Newton, according to an interviewer from the *Economist*, said that one of the pirates spoke perfect English and "was obviously a military officer,"[98] with the implication being that it was a member of one of these anti-piracy units, or at least a member of the Indonesian military. Along this line Jon Vagg has noted that several reports of pirates with military-style crew cuts, clothing, guns, and who spoke good English, thus suggesting military or ex-military personnel.[99] Vagg also describes reports of rigid inflatables being used in several incidents of piracy, typical of military equipment, although definitely not exclusively so. Furthermore, commercial vessels reported seeing smaller ships detaching from a large mother ship and then returning to the same ship on their radar, again possibly suggesting military boats.[100] Other circumstantial evidence comes from interviews with Malaysian security forces conducted by John Burnett for his non-fiction novel *Dangerous Waters*, based on his investigations of piracy in Southeast Asia. Burnett notes Malaysian security personnel reported encounters with TNI forces, described as "lost commands", who claimed to be conducting anti-smuggling activities, but which the Malaysians regarded as a cover for acts of piracy and "shake down" operations.[101] As further anecdotal evidence one security official relates that on a "pirated" boat a 5.56 mm rifle casing was found, "that could have only come from the Indonesian military".[102] Reports like this are not uncommon, and it is widely suspected that the Indonesian military, particularly the Navy, has fallen on hard times from the economic crisis, and is broadening their extra-governmental/extra-legal activities as a result.

International Co-operation: Issues of Security and Sovereignty

International interest in piracy in Southeast Asia is primarily limited to the Singapore and Malacca Straits. The vital economic and strategic nature of these straits as a conduit between the Indian and Pacific Oceans has given piracy there an importance beyond that due to it as a criminal enterprise in itself. Any threat to the sea traffic in this region is taken as a threat to all the sea traffic, and thus as a threat to these international lifelines in general. This is particularly the case over the last several years as many analysts, policy-makers, and people in the media, have theorized links between piracy and terrorism, giving additional weight to piracy as a security threat. An international, multi-lateral approach to addressing piracy might seem ideal, but in practice it is problematic and ultimately comes down to the priority designation given to piracy within regional states. Through this lens the following discussion will look at two international conventions and their attempts to address piracy, and then at issues of multilateral approaches to combating piracy, including security dialogues lead by the Association of Southeast Asian Nations (ASEAN), and the more controversial U.S.-proposed Regional Maritime Security Initiative (RMSI).

Two interrelated issues have been raised concerning the UNCLOS definition of piracy and its applicability to addressing piracy in Southeast Asia. Critics point out that piracy itself has changed significantly since the definition was first drafted, and secondly that with changes to maritime boundaries stemming from articles in UNCLOS, jurisdiction in the seas has significantly changed, affecting the enforcement of piracy according to its definition in Article 101.[103]

Since the UNCLOS definition was first developed nearly fifty years ago the nature of maritime piracy has drastically changed.[104] Notably the incidences of piracy have dramatically increased, especially in territorial waters, where under its own definition piracy cannot exist.[105] Many authors have pointed out that this poses problems for international laws that try to combat maritime piracy, because there is no uniform international law to deal with piracy in territorial waters, and therefore enforcement and prosecution are left to the discretion of the national laws where the incidents take place.[106] This inability to address hotspots of piracy, combined with the increasing frequency of these attacks and their increasing importance as a transnational security threat in the post-Cold War era world geopolitical situation, has caused many to question the use of UNCLOS in addressing piracy.

Another issue that is frequently raised with regard to Article 101 is that even if acts of piracy occur, that is they meet the jurisdictional requirements, the definition restricts piracy to only involving the motive for private gain, i.e. no politically motivated attacks, and it has to involve ship-to-ship conflict. For some who wish to incorporate all maritime violence under the rubric of one term, "piracy", this presents problems because it eliminates maritime terrorism and any crime aboard a ship while in port, although the separation of private and political is positively viewed by this text. These problems taken together — the changing nature of maritime piracy, jurisdictional problems, and restrictions as to which forms of maritime violence are considered piracy — has stimulated much thought about revising the UNCLOS definition.

One such attempt at addressing the perceived inadequacies of the UNCLOS definition and capability for addressing piracy in Southeast Asia is SUA. Despite wide acceptance, however, key maritime Southeast Asian nations such as Indonesia and Malaysia, which closely guard their territorial sovereignty in the Strait of Malacca, have not signed the Convention.[107] Notably the Philippines, Vietnam, Brunei, Myanmar, and Singapore have joined SUA since 2003.[108] Part of this can be explained as pressure from the international community to accede to anti-terrorism

measures as suggested by their only recent ascension, but Singapore's
dependency on international trade and its unique economic and political
conditions also would make it more receptive to this maritime security
convention. Additionally, the promenience of terrorism in track one and
track two security dialogues since September 11, 2001 may have prompted
many countries to reconsider the utility of SUA. SUA's utility in addressing
piracy, however, like UNCLOS is disputed.

While able to sidestep some of the specific requirements of Article
101 in UNCLOS defining piracy, the very broadness of the Convention
makes it less than ideal for addressing the threat of piracy. Article 3 of
SUA could ostensibly be used to address the higher end of piracy,
seizures of entire cargoes or the whole ship itself, but the more common
types of robbery at sea which plague Southeast Asian waters today,
making up the majority of incidents reported, would still be left
unaddressed.[109] Furthermore it has been pointed out that in order to
prosecute crimes under civil law jurisdictions,

> a specific description of the elements of the crime is necessary in order
> to have a valid criminal statute ... in common law jurisdictions, the
> motive for criminal intent must be established ... In both cases, the
> deficiency of the applicable provisions of the SUA represent major
> loopholes for prosecution.[110]

Further problems emerge not just from the structure of the
Convention, but what it would actually imply for those countries who
sign on. Two concerns with SUA are financial obligations and possible
infringements upon national sovereignty. SUA entails a variety of
obligations on signatory states, including information sharing, required
extradition of suspected criminals or prosecution under state laws
"without exception" and "without delay", and "taking all practicable
measures to prevent preparations in their respective territories for the
commission of those offences within or outside their territories".[111]
While there can be few objections to the goals of these requirements,
they could easily entail added expenditure on security that countries
like Indonesia simply do not have to spare, and might also seem to
dictate aspects of internal operations with consideration to law
enforcement and security operations in general, a sensitive topic among
ASEAN nations, making its utility in the Straits region problematic.
There is also concern that SUA could lead to foreign vessels being
allowed to exercise jurisdiction in another country's territorial waters,
which some countries are not yet ready for,[112] and could be seen as a

movement to "internationalize" security in the Straits, which is highly problematic for Indonesia and Malaysia.[113]

Additionally, beyond the requirements of SUA itself there are considerations of whose security agenda does it really address, or simply put, to whose advantage is SUA? Currently the United States is the lone superpower in the world, commanding an economic, political, and military position reminiscent of the British in the nineteenth century. Following terrorist attacks on the World Trade Centre in 2001 the United States has embarked on an aggressive, often unilateral, foreign policy that has led to the overthrow of two predominantly Muslim foreign governments, provoking a massive reinterpretation of international law. Would SUA help countries like Indonesia and Malaysia address issues like piracy? Or would it simply place unwanted economic and political burdens on their shoulders, and increase suspicion of Muslim countries towards the United States? In the nineteenth century piracy afforded colonial powers justification to enter into local affairs and expand their influence. The same process with piracy cum terrorism, and Conventions like SUA, whether intentioned or not, could be interpreted similarly, especially as SUA is being pushed by former colonial powers in the region.

Regional Security, ASEAN, RMSI and Issues of Multilateralism

Given the transnational nature of piracy and its increasing threat, however, there has been a growing awareness by regional states that "unilateral efforts to combat piracy ... are inadequate".[114] Without regional co-operation national borders present a serious challenge to the pursuit and punishment of pirates and any associated criminal networks. Multilateral approaches to piracy and transnational security in general, are important as piracy easily flows across national borders, but these approaches are problematic.

There has been a lot of discussion of piracy in regional security dialogues like ARF (ASEAN Regional Forum) and other ASEAN-based forums, particularly in the context of other transnational crimes such as smuggling and terrorism. However, the relationships between Southeast Asian states in these forums have from their inception generally reflected a strong importance placed on the sovereignty of each state, not to be infringed upon by relations with other states. This includes a tacit understanding that each state will not question or involve itself in the domestic affairs of their regional partners. Traditionally ASEAN has functioned well as an economic forum, but internal politics, human rights, and security concerns are treated with kid gloves, or largely left out of such forums, often being seen as "interventionist".[115] ARF has created a forum where regional and international security issues can be addressed, but internal security issues are generally not topics of discussion, which, until recently, included piracy. In 1978 when the issue of piracy was brought up, "several countries said they regarded the matter as an internal security issue, ending the discussion".[116]

In the early 1990s regional and international pressure stimulated a series of bilateral agreements between Indonesia, Malaysia, Singapore, the Philippines, Thailand,[117] and even Japan,[118] which were very promising in their regional approach. The consequent organization of co-operative anti-piracy patrols between Singapore, Malaysia, and Indonesia appeared to have a dramatic effect in reducing the number of incidents, and shifted the activity away from the Strait of Malacca into the South China Sea.[119] This was widely lauded as an example of successful international co-operation to combat piracy, although there were also allegations that piracy was curtailed because regional governments put their own people in line.[120] These co-operative security efforts were also hampered by sovereignty issues, as "hot pursuit", the actual chasing of suspects, across international boundaries was not allowed. Any real commitment to these patrols seemed to have slipped though, as piracy numbers began to increase in the Strait after a couple of years.

The ASEAN forums have also in recent years brought together various other concerned parties through the ASEAN + 3 forum (ASEAN nations plus China, Japan, and Korea). Efforts in this direction outlined by the:

- 1998 Manila Declaration on the Prevention and Control of Transnational Crime;
- 1999 Joint Communiqué of the Second ASEAN Ministerial Meeting on Transnational Crime;
- 1999 Work Program to Implement the ASEAN Plan of Action to Combat Transnational Crime;
- 2002 Memorandum of Understanding between the Governments of the Member Countries of the Association of Southeast Asian Nations (ASEAN) and the Government of the People's Republic of China on Cooperation in the Field of Non-traditional Security Issues; and
- 2004 Joint Communiqué of The First ASEAN Plus Three Ministerial Meeting on Transnational Crime (AMMTC + 3)

have firmly placed piracy on the regional agenda.[121] Despite the work programme and the action lines regarding piracy, such as information exchange, legal matters, law enforcement, training, and extra-regional co-operation, concretely little seems to have actually been done yet. These forums may be of some utility in generating regional dialogue on piracy as a security matter, but all of these efforts have not produced any lasting deterrents, or created any answers to long-term prevention of piracy.

A fundamental issue in implementing any anti-piracy security stratagem is the sensitive issue of the sovereignty of the littoral states in the straits region, particularly Indonesia. Malaysia, although just as sensitive to perceived or real incursions on its sovereignty, has to all appearances effectively controlled piracy in its maritime territory, as has Singapore, and Singapore's reliance on maritime trade has made them far less contentious on issues of multilateral and international co-operation than either Malaysia or Indonesia.[122] Indonesia, the massive archipelagic nation which controls half of these vital sea lanes, unlike its neighbours, has not managed to effectively control piracy in its waters, and indeed seems to be a weak link in regional maritime security. Despite this unenviable situation Indonesia is not amenable to any measure that might seem to internationalize control of the straits, potentially seen as a "contravention of its territorial sovereignty" in the region.[123]

These frustrations have been compounded as of late since the unveiling of the U.S.-led RMSI to address transnational crime, particularly maritime terrorism, but piracy as well. Coming from outside the ASEAN bloc, being pushed as part of a global security plan by the United States, and the implications for internationalizing the security for the straits region, has raised the hackles of Indonesia and Malaysia. The unilateralist tenor of the initiative also does nothing to appeal to the non-interference, multilateral approach of ASEAN-based security forums. While not endorsing the RMSI, Malaysia and Indonesia, with Singapore (which did support the RMSI) have taken the initial steps towards security co-operation,[124] resulting in co-ordinated trilateral patrols termed "Malsindo" (which stands for Malaysia, Singapore and Indonesia), with other ASEAN nations and India expressing interest in participating.[125] However, from the Indonesian view these patrols may be more to appease the United States and Singapore rather than any real commitment to a joint security initiative, as suggested by the troubling fact that piracy numbers continued to rise despite these patrols, according to Noel Choong, the head of the Piracy Reporting Centre in Kuala Lumpur.[126] In fact, in 2004 the IMB reported thirty-seven attempted and actual attacks, the most ever reported in the Strait of Malacca, the focus of these regional patrols.[127]

Piracy would seem to demand a regional, multilateral approach, but attempts at such avenues while at times promising, have not produced concrete, long-lasting results in either curbing incidents of piracy, or in examining or addressing the root causes of piracy. Co-operative patrols hindered by hot pursuit restrictions, emblematic of sensitive sovereignty issues, are of limited use, and moreover, a focus on co-operative patrols and other policing measures, while important, will not address the economic and political issues within nations that are stimulating piracy. International co-operation through multilateral forums and initiatives are ultimately necessary for dealing with criminal enterprise that can easily, and often does, cross national boundaries. However, international co-operation, even in this "age of globalization", is heavily dependent on the domestic agendas of individual states.

Domestic Priority Designation

The ability of countries to prioritize piracy on their domestic agendas is critical, and the example of Indonesia is illustrative of this. Many of the issues facing Indonesia have already been discussed or mentioned above: secessionist movements also including in West Papua as well as in Aceh, rampant corruption including in the military, uncontrollable maritime borders, illegal fishing that hits the precious coffers of the state and local maritime peoples,[128] ubiquitous smuggling operations that raise issues from lost revenue to controlling the means of violence, organized criminal networks, and of course a range of pirates and pirate gangs operating in Indonesian waters. All of these problems are also put against a backdrop of economic and political turmoil in Indonesia, sparked by Soeharto stepping down in 1998, leaving a gaping political vacuum that needed to be filled not only by new bodies, but by new political ideologies as well. Indonesia is still undergoing extensive political and economic reforms. Issues of decentralization of power, resource distribution, separation of civilian and military spheres of influence, including separating the military from police agencies, has confused and hampered enforcement despite potential long-term benefits of reform.

Serious financial difficulties mean that funding is not available for patrols, equipment, surveillance, and intelligence gathering,[129] which hamper all maritime security efforts including those aimed at piracy. Piracy when viewed in the context of criminal activity in general in

Indonesia may be less significant than IMB statistics may suggest. In Indonesia alone, typically the most pirate-infested waters, there were 1,687 murders reported, approximately 11,000 serious assaults, and approximately 9,000 cases of violent theft in 2002,[130] and the IMB recorded 103 incidents of piracy.[131] Where does Indonesia start? Critically if the matter were left to Indonesia alone the response must ultimately be "not with piracy".

In Indonesian political circles the issue of piracy must seem like an irksome mosquito in a bedroom at night, persistent yet ultimately of little consequence in the short term. Only after several sleepless nights does the annoying mosquito, and concerns of how it came into the bedroom, warrant serious attention. The only attention given to piracy, beyond as a low-level criminal threat, is when it draws unwanted attention, like an outbreak of muggings during tourist season in New York City, or intersects issues of national importance, i.e. the unity of the nation and its sovereignty. So long as Indonesian sovereignty is perceived as not under threat from these activities there can only be minimal expectations of co-operation from them, and the same could be said of Malaysia, although it is not in the piracy "hot seat" right now. Concerns of potential long-term economic damage resulting from the questionable security of their waters and ports, as well as the broader economic and political issues mentioned above that have given rise to piracy, are either of little concern, or are forced to take a back seat to more immediate issues.

Piracy may be a transnational security issue, but it is erupting from certain environments within regional states, so without the *willing and committed* co-operation of Indonesia and other regional states in addressing piracy, little will change in the foreseeable future.

Causative Factors: Historical Continuities and Discontinuities

All of the issues brought up in this section illustrate where there are gaps in the state's ability to control the means of its own legitimacy, primarily the ability to enforce its declared territorial borders, and control the means of violence within those borders. All states face challenges to these facets of their legitimacy, but key states in maritime Southeast Asia, where piracy statistics are the highest of any region in the world, face a broad range of challenges, particularly Indonesia which accounts for a majority of the incidents in Southeast Asia. These challenges create gaps in the political hegemony of the state, from which piracy emerges and which piracy itself serves to widen; like an invasive weed it creates a habitat suitable to its own survival and those weeds of a similar ilk. The low-level criminal threat of piracy has intersected with issues of international concern as it threatens the economic and militarily strategic security of vital sea ways in the region. This international concern and attention given to piracy has in turn made piracy an important issue for Indonesia, where it might otherwise have received little priority in a domestic agenda riddled with much higher priority concerns.

There is much continuity between the gaps in political hegemony of states contemporarily and historically that allowed piracy to emerge and flourish. The physical and cultural geography of the region make enforcing any state's power and authority problematic. Moreover, enforcing maritime boundaries historically was simply beyond local states not interested in this project, and beyond the means of colonial powers This was especially the case in times of relative weakness such as the late eighteenth and early to mid-nineteenth century, where scant resources were not available to effectively patrol or protect much of the maritime world. This began to change by the end of the nineteenth century as technological developments by colonial powers, which will be discussed in more detail in the following section, allowed the tightening of borders and simultaneously expanded and quickened the pace of imperial expansion. However, this does not mean that the ideal of total control was ever reached by colonial states, and boundaries established by these powers are still contested contemporarily. The sheer scale of maritime territory ostensibly under the control of modern maritime states in Southeast Asia has made it difficult if not impossible to physically manage and maintain the integrity of their territorially defined authority. Indonesia's porous boundaries in an environment antithetical to proscriptions of rigid territoriality, combined with the inability to enforce them, is a major gap in state control, which pirates and other non-state actors are quick to exploit.

The permeability of these borders and its relationship to maritime crime is highlighted by the perennial and widespread existence of smuggling. As long as there has been any kind of trade restriction that has made illegal commerce profitable, smuggling has existed. Tagliacozzo describes smuggling operations carried out across Dutch and British borders, noting the "facility with which contrabanders were able to procure weapons cargos always seemed to keep pace with the state's designs to improve its own interdiction capabilities".[132] Smuggling of firearms through porous borders was of constant concern to the colonial authorities, as it is today with state authorities, and represented a serious potential threat to their hegemony. Both in the past and presently, smuggling has also been an enabling factor of piracy. The illegal trade networks built around smuggled goods provide potential market links for pirate rings, with which they can unload their booty, as well as acquire materials, like guns or anything else they need. Even if smuggling only infrequently deals with "pirated" goods, these networks have created markets willing to deal in "questionable" goods.

These networks have in part also facilitated overt challenges to the state. If geography and smuggling are the back alleyways by which piracy operates, networks of small gaps in a state's political hegemony, insurrections like those in Aceh and Mindanao create gaps like four-lane highways. These movements put entire regions beyond the authority and power of the state, leaving room for piracy to operate. A similar process can be seen in the historical case studies of piracy. All the examples provided in some way capitalized on political instability in the region. The Bugis's move into the Malay world was sparked by wars in their homelands and facilitated by political instability in the Malay world itself. The Chinese/Vietnamese example arose from an insurrection in Vietnam and was able to spread into southern China in part due to rebellions in other parts of China that drew away resources and took priority over piracy. To some degree the Iban and Iranun expansion in the eighteenth and nineteenth century was sparked by political instability, as the decline of the Sultanate of Brunei coupled with British intervention in the region helped escalate the raiding traditions of the Iban. The Iranun were able to be so successful in large part because of the general instability of the region, including in the Dutch, British, and Spanish spheres of influence.

Patronage of piracy and the prevalence of non-state actors operating beyond state control is a key component affecting piracy, and negatively affecting a state's political hegemony. Contemporarily, although the patrons of piracy are not always clear, the role they play is similar as their pre-colonial counterparts. The patronage of piracy both in the past and present is not 100 per cent necessary for piracy to exist, but is necessary for organizing any large-scale forays. Patronage in part extends from the pervasiveness of patron–clientilism in the region. The personalized, flexible power structures were essentially how historic, indigenous states functioned. The charismatic leader was at the centre of the state and controlled various commodities such as wealth, potency, and prestige, with which he would extend his personal network of influence. Similarly, today this system operates within and around the meritocracy of the modern state bureaucracy, creating space for personal influence as easily within the local harbour as in the national assembly. The legitimacy of such patronage has changed significantly, however, and is now part of widespread corruption.

In the past when piracy or raiding was an intrinsic element of state structures, and therefore often received their support, the scale of the excursions could be massive. Today when piracy connects with organized crime and/or the tacit support, or wilful negligence at least, of the state, high-end piracy is possible. Without this patronage piracy is largely an ad hoc organization of low-end hit-and-run sea robberies. Patronage, and state complicity especially, give piracy a sense of legitimacy, creating independent loci of power that are gaps in the state's hegemonic control of power. In the past when states or rulers could no longer guarantee the safety of their ports, trade would divert to competitors, thus further weakening these trade-dependent states. Contemporarily states like Indonesia are not so dependent on trade (although Singapore is), but their economy could suffer from a similar lack of confidence in the state's abilities to maintain security.

International co-operation was and is an important element of Westphalian states in curbing piracy, or curbing indigenous forms of competitive maritime behaviour. Historically, when international relations between colonial powers in the region were non-cooperative due to economic and political competition with each other, piracy had room to operate. The British would turn a blind eye on Iranun raids if they were in Dutch territory, just as raids in any competitor's sphere of influence would be of little concern. Until the British, Dutch, and Spanish could all commit to making piracy a priority in their agendas, once they were entrenched colonial powers and it was in their own interests to help create the means of a stable economic environment, piracy continued to operate. This is evinced by the Iranun raids that continued well into the second half of the nineteenth century in the region. Contemporarily, regional states like Indonesia are still very much engaged in establishing their sphere of influence, competing with neighbours economically, politically, and in some cases territorially, even competing against former colonial powers. This process has handicapped efforts at international co-operation to address piracy and is a major gap that piracy is able to exploit.

In the nineteenth century, as today, ultimately it is the ability of regional states to give priority to the issue of piracy that will bring it back under control. Also as in the nineteenth century this is not necessarily an easy task. Britain, the Netherlands, and Spain faced various critical issues in their domestic agendas that prevented them from giving priority to the issue of piracy, including a lack of will to address the issue based on the financial bottom line. Indonesia is the hotspot of piracy in Southeast Asia for largely the same reason. There are more important demands for resources and political attention than the issue of piracy. It is only when piracy is perceived to intersect with priority issues of national stability that it even gets token priority.

TOOLS, INTELLIGENCE, TACTICS, AND COMPLIMENTARY TECHNOLOGY

This section is focused on practical causative factors of pirate attacks, discussing what has given pirates an advantage vis-à-vis their targets and the state, contemporarily and in the past, and in part explain the resurgence of piracy. This balance of power is constituted in part by access to and efficient use of available tools, and for this discussion will primarily include weapons and boats. The balance of power between pirates and the state is further looked at through the control of intelligence, including information technology, and tactical knowledge as it pertains to either carrying out acts of piracy, or in curtailing them. The analysis of each of these, and the interaction between these three security commodities, will be framed in terms of "complimentary technology", using tools, intelligence and tactical knowledge to bring available technology to bear with maximum effect. Contemporarily pirates have the initiative in this dynamic balance of power, as they once did in the past as well. In the final section of this chapter this discussion will provide a brief summary and analyse the previous discussions through historical context, particularly making use of the Iranun case study. This will demonstrate the utility of complimentary technology and its role in facilitating piracy in the past as well as the present, and how this advantage can be addressed.

Weapons

There are two types of weapons typically used by pirates in Southeast Asia — knives and light arms. Knives, including machetes and their Malay-Indonesian counterpart *parangs*, are common weapons of pirates, in part because of their prevalence but also because the use of guns often carry far more jail time.[133] Despite their prevalence and potential deadliness, however, they are of little concern for this discussion because they are common throughout the region as a household tool, being legally owned. Light arms on the other hand are of much more concern, being illegal in much if not all of the region, posing serious potential threats to state security forces as well as to the targets of pirates.

Access to this weaponry has helped to level the technological playing field between pirates and the state apparatus, posing a serious threat to any state's claim to monopolizing the means of violence. Chalk points out that the term "light arms" is a misnomer, for in this category are assault rifles like the M-16 and AK-47 that are capable of discharging a thirty-round clip in three seconds, all manner of hand guns, rocket-propelled grenades able to penetrate 330mm of armour, and even land mines, all of which have a "phenomenal capacity to kill and inflict chaos and mayhem".[134] It is their light weight and easy portability that makes them "light arms", ideal for military operations, or piracy. These weapons are currently still being widely mass produced, and tens of millions already exist in the world, making them widely available and relatively cheap.[135] Many of the arms available in Southeast Asia are the result of Cold War tensions being played out, where millions of tons of military hardware were poured into countries like Cambodia, Vietnam, the Philippines, Afghanistan, Pakistan, and numerous African countries.[136] An article from *The Australian* reported in the late 1970s that around the southern Philippines: "Armed with heavy weapons left over from the Indochina war, the pirates were halting fishing boats, yachts, coastal steamers and even small ocean-going freighters on the high seas and taking their cargo and possessions."[137] After the end of the Cold War, militaries began to reduce in size and started to unload millions of pieces of hardware that were no longer needed. Additionally, with the collapse of the Soviet Union and several associated Communist states in Eastern Europe, these countries were looking for sources of hard currency, and one thing they had to sell was military hardware. As a commodity on the market it unfortunately has many willing buyers.

These weapons are being used in numerous pirate attacks, and even John Burnett reported in his book that when his yacht was attacked by pirates they were carrying M-16 rifles.[138] Not all pirate attacks involve these kinds of weapons, as they are still comparatively expensive in poorer countries like Indonesia, where part-time fishermen-turned-pirates could not afford such hardware.[139] Their use generally suggests the involvement of more connected patrons that have access to, and can afford, these weapons, such as organized crime or rogue state actors. Furthermore, because the use of firearms carries more jail time their use would also suggest an immediate escalation in the risk-return, violence, organization scale, or that there was no expectation of getting caught.

Having firearms also dictates an advantage over most commercial vessels as the majority of private ships do not carry arms, as they could provoke an escalation in violence that could threaten both crew and volatile cargoes, although it is up to each shipping company to make its own regulations.[140] Carrying firearms would also be difficult as they must navigate a variety of national waters where arms may be illegal, and might cause unwanted hassle and delays once in port.

These weapons are not the cause of piracy, but they provide the pirates who can afford them with the means of violence equivalent to most state security forces, thus allowing them to carry out their attacks with greater confidence. On a broader level, the presence of these arms in such quantities represents a serious failure of regional states to control the means of violence within their territories, and it also represents a skewed global community that has allowed these weapons to become a frequent commodity of trade.

Vessels

Pirate attacks typically require a boat of some kind from which to launch their attack, particularly if the target is a moving vessel. In a maritime environment where fishing and sea-borne trade are economic mainstays, boats are not hard to come by. Typical sleek, wood-hulled fishing vessels, sea worthy beyond the immediate shoreline, with two or three powerful outboard engines dropped in for speed, seem to be a constant presence in reported pirate attacks.[141] These boats are more than capable of catching tankers, freighters, or fishing vessels on the move. The actual type of vessel is largely irrelevant, although the wooden structure may actually hide the boat from radar,[142] and the common use of locally produced boats does suggest a local origin of the pirates using them. Importantly, pirates can consistently field boats capable of carrying out their attacks.

Police and commercial vessels, however, are not as flexible as pirates are in their choice or access to suitable boats for catching or dissuading pirates. For example, Burnett describes a conversation with Malaysian maritime police where the police had just gotten new, faster boats to keep pace with local pirates. Burnett continues: "That superiority, however, would only last a few weeks. Local gangs ... got wind of the police escalation and built sleeker fibreglass and wood boats; and they added two more engines that gave them eight hundred horses [horse power]."[143] In Malaysia at least, as the police enhance their capabilities, the pirates do as well.

The biggest limitation in the selection of boats, beyond what is immediately practical, is money. In this respect pirates have a distinct advantage over the police. The pirates are not hindered by the same bureaucratic hurdles in acquiring or spending funds as the police are, so that they can obtain new equipment far more quickly than the police, and their budgetary considerations are far more narrowly defined. This is particularly the case with security forces in Indonesia that have faced massive budgetary cuts since the economic crisis of the last few years. This would also apply to commercial vessels of all types, particularly large freighters and tankers. In private industry boat technology has actually indirectly encouraged piracy, and then had to find ways to discourage it. These vessels are built to convey goods as efficiently and cheaply as possible, generally on very tight profit margins, and not necessarily designed to repel or outrun pirates. Also the mobility of commercial vessels is often quite restricted, with top speeds of only 10–15 knots in open seas, and often less in busy straits as traffic increases. Increasing automation of freighters has reduced the number of people needed to operate the ship, thus saving money in wages and associated costs, but fewer people on board means an easier target for pirates, with fewer eyes able to keep a look out, and fewer people to subdue.[144] Some shipping companies have started investing in anti-piracy devices, however, such as the Secure-Ship electric fence advertised at the IMB website,[145] and GPS (global positioning system) to track the vessels' movements,[146] and/or resorted to more cost-effective methods such as fire hoses,[147] and security lights,[148] to deter boardings. Repelling intruders must come down to the bottom line of a cost benefit analysis. Smaller craft like local fishing boats and traders are even more restricted in their choices, as their financial capacities are often extremely limited, as well as practical considerations of the smooth functioning of the boat.

These anti-piracy devices have been successful in dissuading opportunist pirates, but it is unlikely they would be able to dissuade a determined assault, such as high-end attacks on the *Petro Ranger* or *Tenyu*. The scale of potential pay-off versus associated risks for the pirates appears to be a linear trend, while the cost benefit analysis of shipping companies and security flattens out as the bottom line of profitability is reached.

The pirates have customized their boats to their needs while their targets are simply not able to customize their vessels to repel pirates. The boat race between pirates and the police is still waiting for the finish, but with budgetary and bureaucratic constraints for the police, pirates in the near future at least look like they are ahead. Of more importance than who has the faster boat, however, is who knows where the boat is coming from or going to.

Intelligence

For this discussion, intelligence will include a range of information under the rubric of "local knowledge", details of local conditions, geography, targets, and movements of people. Not just the nature of the information, but the local element that is providing the information is of importance. Intelligence will also cover information technology such as GPS, radar, cell phones, and the Internet that provide information and organizational capabilities.

For low-end piracy local knowledge is likely the only intelligence available and/or necessary to pirates preying in their home waters, or their nearby neighbour's. Any maritime-oriented person or group would already have detailed knowledge of the geography, targets such as fishermen, local traders, or even passing international commercial traffic in the sea lanes just off the coast, as well as knowledge of the police, their movements, habits and corruptibility. They would know the best place to ambush ships, or to lay low after an attack, or where to take their goods afterward, and who was to be trusted and who was not. Each local pirate or gang would instinctively take advantage of this intelligence.

The presence of these local "experts" in the various hotspots of piracy in the region, from the Malacca Strait to the Sulu Sea, are also likely important for high-end organized piracy rings that operate on a regional basis. In an area as socially, politically, and geographically complex as maritime Southeast Asia, the use of local recruits would be of particular value, and are a likely pool of recruits on which these organizations draw. These informants can be strategically placed or recruited to provide information concerning specific shipments of goods, route details, ship layout, and crew rotations. Sometimes it may be as simple as bribing a port official,[149] or finding a ship's crew member who needs extra money, and not even necessarily finding local pirates. There is also the use of unwilling, local sources of intelligence, i.e. hostages. Frequently hostages are taken by pirates, even if only temporarily, while they ransack the vessel.[150] Hostages are often forced to provide information about the locations of valuables, the nature of the cargo, and any specific information needed by the pirates.

The use of IT has become standard throughout much of the world, including with pirates in Southeast Asia. Dupont has observed that "globalizing forces of the information age are transforming the way in which criminals organize and operate".[151] Criminal gangs utilize cellular technology to keep track of their informants who can relay a target's position in real time, or they can gain access to Internet sites that ship owners use to track their ships via satellite GPS systems (ironically to help prevent losing ships), and know almost exactly where the ship is.[152] Radar is a ubiquitous feature on freighters of any size, and an important navigational tool, as well as a potential anti-piracy tool.[153] Radar can also be used by state security forces for similar purposes, but it can just as easily be used by pirates trying to track ships as they pick targets, or to evade pursuers.[154]

Beyond tactical considerations IT also allows for more efficient organization across distances, allowing syndicates to operate without a home base, making them difficult to track. E-banking through the Internet has also facilitated money laundering across national boundaries by criminal groups, while police and security forces must respect the lines of national sovereignty, making it difficult to trace transactions.[155] Moreover, simply the sheer number of transactions that can be made electronically can hide potentially vast profits of organized crime,[156] including those from piracy. Certainly not all pirates have access to the latest IT, or need of it, but many of the more organized gangs would have access to these technologies. IT simply allows a more efficient, faster organization of information, which pirates, commercial shippers, and security forces can take advantage of. The question is less who has access to IT, but who is able to make the best use of it, or is able to afford it.

Tactics and Complimentary Technology

There are a myriad of tactics used by pirates to gain access to ships, reflective of the diversity of means and objectives of the pirates. Some attacks occur in broad daylight, others on nights with no moon. Some attacks only involve knives and clubs, while others involve assault rifles and grenades. This discussion is not meant as an exhaustive list of tactics used, but rather as a general demonstration of why their tactics are effective. The reason they are effective is because they use the tools, intelligence, and tactics to form a complimentary technology to their target's and pursuer's weaknesses.

State security forces are notably weak against guerilla tactics, as they cannot police everywhere all the time, and they do not have the ability to monitor every boat on the water. As mentioned above this is particularly the case with the massive maritime territories of archipelagic states coupled with weak economies not able to fund adequate security. Pirates seem able to monitor security forces in a way that the police appear not to be able to monitor pirates. In this way pirates can pick their opportunities, either through extensive preparation and planning, or simply through observation and patience. Pirates can pose as fishermen, or are indeed fishermen at least part-time, and can blend in and raconteur potential targets,[157] or even use it as a ruse to lure in unsuspecting vessels.[158] While in many cases this is simply a factor of the pirates literally being part of the crowd, it could also be a conscious tactic to avoid detection, allowing pirates to stay active in busy waters like the Straits region, the South China Sea, and the Sulu Sea.

When attacking a vessel pirates can use a ruse as mentioned above, or can rely on stealth and surprise. A typical account of an attack on a moving vessel would involve a local wooden fishing vessel or boat outfitted with large engines for speed, using a moonless night and/or rough seas to avoid detection from the deck watch and/or radar respectively. For a larger vessel like a freighter or tanker they would approach from the stern, taking advantage of a possible radar shadow, depending on the radar, and avoiding the worst of the wake from the ship's engine. The pirates can then bring their boat in close and the displaced water from the wake can actually draw the boat up against the target.[159] From here pirates would use a grappling hook gun, or home-made variety, or even bamboo poles tied together (depending on the height of the vessel) with a hook, to gain the deck. From there, depending greatly on the intent of the attack, the attackers would grab what they could and scramble overboard, hopefully surprise the captain and crew and hold them hostage while ransacking the boat, kidnap officers for ransom, or round up the crew with intent of eventually disposing of them somehow. The latter three often involve threatening or physically harming crew members to intimidate and control the rest of the crew.

All this is relative to the target and the nature of the attack. Attacks are often thwarted by simply removing the element of surprise, using alarm systems, spotlights, watching the radar, and having simple anti-piracy devices in action such as fire hoses. Pirates typically look for the most vulnerable targets — fishermen, local traders, and unprepared larger commercial vessels. Pirates would not likely attack a military vessel, or otherwise secure ship, for the risk return ratio would be far out of proportion.

Pirates are able to use the tools available to them, in concert with the intelligence available to them, to create flexible tactics of operation that work against a diversity of targets. This suite of tools, intelligence, and tactics creates a total complimentary technology that allows pirates to hit and run, evade capture, and live freely to engage in further piracy.

Causative Factors: Historical Continuities and Discontinuities

Presently, the situation is similar to the earlier half of the nineteenth century. As in the past, pirates today make use of available tools, adaptive strategies, flexible organization, singular goals, local knowledge, and tactics, to create a complimentary technology to take advantage of the weaknesses in their targets, and of those security forces charged with stopping them. Pirates have access to the boats they need, weapons, intelligence and information technology that the state no longer controls access to, and/or is not able to claim a monopoly over.

In terms of tools, little can be done to prevent speed boats from falling into the hands of pirates, but restricting access to firearms and promoting the development of domestic patrol capacities will reduce the capabilities of pirates and restrict their operational spaces. The real focus, however, needs to be on intelligence, both in developing or utilizing intelligence networks, and in controlling the flow of information to the pirates. Historically, one of the primary advantages raiders had was knowledge of trade routes, settlement patterns and local holidays (to predict people's movements), fishing grounds (where food could be found, and there were fishing boats to be plundered), as well as geographical details of river systems, currents, and reefs, important for navigating, making an ambush or facilitating a getaway. Groups came by this information in two primary ways, through personal experience and from using local people. Experience taught many of these things, but making use of local recruits, or locals captured for slaves, provided detailed knowledge of specific areas.[160] The destruction of Iranun raiding bases was made possible not just by steam ships, but by local informants who took the Spanish to these bases.[161] This is a vital element of pirates' complimentary technology, just as it was in the past.

Over the last few decades globalization has dramatically expanded access to technology and information networks, connecting regions of the world more intimately than ever before. While modern means of gathering and disseminating information have become more sophisticated since the days of light beacons and telegraphs, they are no longer the sole possession of the state, and are widely available to anyone with the resources and basic knowledge of their workings. These networks have been largely outside state control, and have created new opportunities for criminal organizations to operate across national boundaries. In this case the cliché "knowing is half the battle" aptly fits the contemporary situation.

Similar to contemporary pirates, historic pirate/raiders tools, intelligence and tactics made them flexible and adaptable. Like their modern counterparts they would take advantage of their target's weaknesses and vulnerability, attacking a ship becalmed at night near to shore, kidnapping lone fishermen or women washing their clothes at the river or beach, or even taking advantage of the minimal, or non-existent, defences of the Spanish Philippines and besiege entire towns.[162] Contemporarily pirates can hide in the background of the busy waterways of Southeast Asia, posing as fishermen, and/or use a variety of tactics to catch their targets and their would-be pursuers off guard. In the past pirates took advantage of the fact that states had no effective way of monitoring the vast stretches of seas in their spheres of influence, and the state didn't know who to look for or where to look for them, similar as today. It was only through a combination of the expansion of their political control, increasing intelligence capabilities, and new tools of empire, that they brought raiding states to heel and successfully imposed their political will and legal codes on much of the region. Thus forcing another metamorphosis and adaptation of piracy/raiding, to something similar to what exists today. Total security will never be achieved in the maritime realm, but if states can better control the tools and intelligence of pirates, they will take away the tactical advantages, and thus the entire suite of complimentary technology of pirates (as states eventually managed to do in the past), and they will be able to more effectively control the scope and frequency of attacks.

In the past piracy was brought under control at a point when the complimentary technology of the raiders/pirates was made obsolete in the face of the expanding empires. The sophistication and security capabilities of colonial states, in all the categories discussed, was far beyond that available to raiders. Yet, even at this time piracy persisted, albeit in drastically reduced scope and frequency. As history suggests, piracy will never disappear entirely, but it is up to contemporary states to do what they can to control it. Much of this must be done at the level of economic development, political and policy reform, dependent upon the will of governments, but concrete steps can be taken to *prevent* piracy based on the previous discussion.

CHAPTER SUMMARY

In the last thirty years piracy has reappeared on the media radar, and in the last fifteen years has become a serious security concern in maritime Southeast Asia. There are a number of continuities with conditions and challenges faced by regional states today as were faced by their colonial and indigenous progenitors. There is continuity of a maritime socio-cultural matrix that still practises a broad-based subsistence economy, of which piracy is still a "thinkable" component. Contemporarily piracy is emerging from these old centres of maritime power; places where contemporarily maritime peoples live in subsistence-level poverty or worse, have been marginalized from the territorially (terra firma) defined nations and national identities. These states have their centres of power, prestige, and money far from the coastal tracks from which they still try to eke out a meagre living, similar to the Vietnamese/Chinese piracy case study. The state has not been able to effectively redistribute the wealth, a situation made worse by the recent economic crisis, and thus has failed to exercise a key state control on piracy. Without a legitimate stake in the growing economy, and/or a constructive role in a national identity, there is a temptation to seek alternative access through piracy, much as happened periodically in the past.

These problems are in part created, and exacerbated, by weak state control of political hegemony, i.e. the means of a state's legitimacy: monopolistic control over violence within defined territorial borders. Numerous gaps in this control have allowed piracy the operational space to re-emerge, and piracy is actively widening these gaps as well. Similar to the challenge that faced the colonial states, the modern littoral states of Southeast Asia are responsible for securing vast sea spaces, made even larger by changes to maritime territorial definitions in UNCLOS. Long-standing traditions of cultural geography that link the region via the maritime realm also further complicate enforcement of these defined territorial boundaries. Mass movements of people across these seascapes contemporarily, demonstrated by the flow of Vietnamese refugees, the movement of Bajau, and even labour migration in the wake of the economic crisis, all highlight the difficulties of enforcing the porous maritime boundaries in Southeast Asia. Similar to the colonial era, smugglers utilize this vast maritime space, taking advantage of the "rigid" boundaries that have generated tariff and price differentials and complicate legal enforcement. They help create markets for illegal goods and provide access to firearms for pirates, as well as regional separatist movements. While the maritime activities of these separatist movements are not piracy, the gaps in security, the resources they drain from other security efforts, and the market for smuggled goods and weapons they help generate, create major gaps in the political hegemony of regional states that piracy can take advantage of. As seen from the case studies, political instability creates opportunities for piracy to emerge and flourish beyond state control.

Patronage of piracy is, and has been, an important element in shaping the scope of piracy, and today creates a large gap in the political hegemony of regional states. While not necessary for piracy to exist, it was instrumental in allowing large-scale raids in the past, and is instrumental in high-end organized piracy today. This patronage is in part made possible by the long tradition of patron-clientilism, a basic element of many socio-cultural-political systems in the region, which is still present and active today. These systems create spaces for personal influence that in turn can give rise to corruption within the state structure, providing access to support, direct or indirect, from the state, and create a widespread informal power structures suited for behind-the-scenes power brokerage. Today, any patronage of piracy, or predatory maritime violence, is illegitimate, unlike in the past, and is particularly problematic when the state is implicated in supporting these activities. When power and wealth accrues to non-state actors such as pirates and their patrons, this in effect legitimizes these criminal acts, and at the same time contravenes the legitimacy of the state.

Also similar to the past, regional and extra-regional states with interests in the region are engaged in economic, territorial and political competition, which is complicating co-operative efforts to address piracy. Moreover, serious domestic issues faced by these states, particularly seen in Indonesia, make it difficult to prioritize or effectively deal with piracy.

Furthermore, the complimentary technology of pirates contemporarily, as in the nineteenth century, is able to effectively take advantage of the weaknesses of their targets and security forces. The limited capacity of state security forces, as with colonial powers through much of the nineteenth century, provides pirates with space to manoeuvre and surprise their targets without immediate response by the authorities. This is in large part possible because pirates have access to better intelligence regarding local knowledge of geography, tactical details of their targets, movements of security forces and the like. Contemporarily this also reflects the ability of pirates to make use of expanding global information networks and various information technologies to their advantage, providing greater organizational capacity and potentially greater tactical detail. Low-end ad hoc piracy largely functions without need of these networks, as their local knowledge provides sufficient intelligence for their needs. However, these information tools and networks are vital for high-end organized piracy which may need to organize on a regional scale.

All of these factors taken together have created an environment that provides motivation, rationalization, means, and opportunities in which piracy can exist and flourish.

Notes

1. The term "maritime peoples" will generally be understood to include anyone with nautical skills, or who earns a significant part of their living from the sea, and/or their personal or community identity is intimately linked to the maritime realm.
2. Jonathan Rigg, *Southeast Asia: The Human Landscape of Modernization and Development*, 2nd ed. (London: Routledge, 2003), p. 330.
3. Ibid., pp. 321–38.
4. Rizal Sukma, "The Security Problematique of Globalization and Development: The Case of Indonesia", in *Development and Security in Southeast Asia*, edited by David B. Dewitt and Carolina G. Hernandez, *Globalization*, vol. 3 (Hants, England: Ashgate Publishing Company, 2003), p. 242.
5. Hadi Soesastro, "Globalization, Development, and Security in Southeast Asia: An Overview", in *Development and Security in Southeast Asia*, edited by Dewitt and Hernandez, *Globalization* vol. 3, p. 22.
6. Rigg, *Southeast Asia*, p. 163.
7. Yonhap, "Global Shipping Industry Expects another Boom Year", *Asia Pulse*, 7 January 2004, Sec. Northern Territory Regional.
8. World Trade Organization News Press Release, Press/386, 25 October 2004, http://www.wto.org/english/news_e/pres04_e/pr386_e.htm (accessed 21 February 2005).

9. World Trade Organization, http://www.wto.org/english/thewto_e/minist_e/min96_e/maritime.htm (accessed 27 March 2004).

10. "TNI AL Siap Hadapi Pembajakan di Laut" [TNI AL is Ready to Face Piracy at Sea], *Kompas*, 29 June 2001, http://www.kompas.com/kompas-cetak/0106/29/jatim/tnia46.htm (accessed 27 March 2004).

11. T. Yulianti, "Bajak Laut" [Pirates], *Suara Pembaruan Daily*, 13 June 2003, p. 2 of 4, printout from online, http://mail2.factsoft.de/pipermail/national/2002-June/005671.html (accessed 27 March 2004).

12. Jason Abbot and Neil Renwick, "Pirates? Maritime Piracy and Societal Security in Southeast Asia", *Pacifica Review* 11, no. 1 (February 1999): 15.

13. *Food and Agriculture Organization of the United Nations* (FAO), http://www.fao.org/fi/fcp/fcp.asp (accessed 27 March 2004).

14. Ibid.

15. According to FAO statistics in countries like the Philippines and Indonesia, the majority of fishing is done by unpowered small boats, 53.6 per cent in Indonesia and in the Philippines 90 per cent of vessels were under 150 gross tons (small boats). Furthermore, in Indonesia the majority were part-timers, i.e. supplementing their incomes in other ways. This indicates a predominance of small-scale operations, and suggests a marginal lifestyle from fishing.

16. Abbot and Renwick, "Pirates?", p. 21.

17. See Brian Fegan, "Plundering the Sea", *Inside Indonesia*, January–March 2003, pp. 1–2 of 5 on printout, http://www.insideindonesia.org/edit73/Fegan%20fishing.htm (accessed 2 February 2005). Fegan writes that Thai fishing operations in the Arafura Sea around Papua have been known to use steel rollers to crush reefs and then scour the area with nets in order to catch everything they can, maximizing the bio-mass of the catch.

18. James Francis Warren, "A Tale of Two Centuries", ARI Working Thesis, no. 2, June 2003, http://www.ari.nus.edu.sg/pub/wps2003.htm (accessed 27 March 2004).

19. Maritime peoples engaging in piracy also further risk their own and others livelihoods, as the majority of victims are fishermen and other typically poor maritime people, and increase the risk of environmental catastrophe in the region.

20. Alan Dupont, *East Asia Imperiled: Transnational Challenges to Security* (Cambridge: Cambridge University Press, 2001), p. 103.

21. "How Not to Deter Refugees; By Allowing Them to be Killed by Pirates", *The Economist*, sec. World Politics and Current Affairs, U.S. ed., p. 16, *LexisNexis Academic* online database.

22. Sethuraman Dinakar, "The Jolly Roger Flies High … As Piracy Feeds the Hungary", *Business Week International Editions*, vol. 3630, 24 May 1999, sec. Spotlight on the Strait of Malacca, p. 4.

23. See Rigg, *Southeast Asia*, pp. 111–14, and the whole volume in general for

a good discussion of the effects, both imagined and real, of rapid economic development in Southeast Asia.

24. BPS, Statistics Indonesia (BPS, Badan Pusat Statistiks, or Central Statistics Bureau), http://www.bps.go.id/index.shtml (accessed 28 March 2004). Unemployment increased in Indonesia by almost two million people, or approximately a 30 per cent increase between 1997 and 1999 (excluding Maluku Province where statistics were not available).

25. Philippines National Statistics Office, http://www.census.gov.ph/ (accessed 27 March 2004). In the ARMM, of which the Sulu Archipelago is a part, the magnitude of poverty has increased from approximately 1,300,000 (54 per cent) to 1,700,000 (70 per cent) between 1997 and 2000, in a region where the total population is 2,400,000.

26. See Warren, "Tale of Two Centuries", pp. 16–19; William M. Carpenter and David G. Wiencek, "Maritime Piracy in Asia", in *Asian Security Handbook*, edited by Carpenter and Wiencek (New York: Armonk, 2000), p. 89; "Piracy Resurgence", *The Australian*, 8 November 1978, p. 11; Ralph Johnstone, "The Sea Gypsies", *AsiaWeek*, 21 April 1993.

27. Leslie Geen, *The Authority of the State* (Oxford: Clarendon Press, 1988), pp. 83–84.

28. See Appendix A for further explanation of the EEZ in the description of UNCLOS, and later in this chapter for discussions of the EEZ in relation to piracy.

29. For example, see Cynthia Chou, "Contesting the Tenure of Territoriality", *Bijdragen tot de Taal-, Land- en Volkenkunde* 153, no. 4 (1997); Clifford Sather, *The Bajau Laut* (Kuala Lumpur: Oxford University Press, 1997); and Johnstone, "The Sea Gypsies".

30. Sather, *Bajau Laut*, p. 54.

31. Ibid., pp. 87–89.

32. Orang Laut is a general name applied to dozens of individual, sea going ethnic groups in the waters around the Riau-Lingga Archipelago. The author recognizes this distinction, but for the sake of this discussion the name will be used in its generic sense to refer to these peoples in a collective sense.

33. Carl A. Trocki, *Prince of Pirates* (Singapore: Singapore University Press, 1979), p. xix.

34. See, for example, C.A. Gibson-Hill, "The Orang Laut of the Singapore River and the Sampan Panjang", *Royal Asiatic Society Journal Malayan Branch* XXV, Pt. 1 (1952): 161–74; Chou, "Contesting the Tenure of Territoriality"; Mubyarto, "Riau Progress and Poverty", translated by Robson, Chou, and Derks, *Bijdragen tot de Taal-, Land- en Volkekunde* 153, no. 4 (1997): 542–56; Cathy A. Hoshour, "Resettlement and the Politicization of Ethnicity in Indonesia", *Bijdragen Tot de Taal-, Land en Volkekunde* 153, no. 4 (1997): 557–76; Barbara Watson-Andaya, "Recreating a Vision", *Bijdragen Tot de*

Taal-, Land en Volkekunde 153, no. 4 (1997): 483–507; Lioba Lenhart, "Ethnic Minority Policy and National Development in Indonesia", in *Nationalism and Ethnicity in Southeast Asia*, edited by Ingrid Wessel (Munster, Germany: Lit Verlag, 1993), pp. 577–604.

35. Andaya, B.W., "Recreating a Vision", p. 505.

36. In the period 1870–1910, prior to which large-scale raids were still emanating from Sulu, Tagliacozzo notes that piracy still persisted, albeit in significantly changed form (Eric Tagliacozzo, *Secret Trades of the Straits: Smuggling and State-formation along a Southeast Asian Frontier, 1870-1910* [Hartford: Yale University Press, 1999], pp. 244–45). A. G. Course, in *Pirates of the Eastern Seas* (London: Cox and Lyman Limited, 1966), p. 1, relates that pirates were still operating between the two world wars and as late as 1961, and furthermore in the 1950s and 60s Vagg has reported that inter-village raids still occurred. We also know that following the exodus of Vietnamese boat people starting in 1975, there were numerous acts of piracy, bringing us to the last fifteen years when incidents of piracy are not infrequently reported in the media.

37. Jon Vagg, "Rough Seas?", *British Journal of Criminology* 35, no. 1 (1995): 67.

38. Ibid., p. 68.

39. Abbot and Renwick, "Pirates?", p. 20.

40. "Nelayan Belawan Takut Melaut" [Fishermen from Belawan are Afraid to go to Sea], SCTV 6, 26 June 2003, sec. Laporan Daerah, http://www.liputan6.com/fullnews/59141.html (accessed 27 February 2004). *Kompas* also has a good online archive that revealed several mentions of piracy and these local targets. Following are three of the most recent articles: "Selat Bangka Masih Rawan Perompakan" [Southern Bangka Still Troubled by Piracy], 17 November 2004, http://www.kompas.com (accessed 13 January 2005); "TNI AL Tangkap Otak Perompakan Dua Kapal Asing di Natuna" [Indonesian Navy Arrests Pirate Mastermind of Two Foreign Ships in Natuna], 8 August 2004, http://www.kompas.com (accessed 13 January 2005); "Polisi Tangkap Kawanan Perompak Nelayan di Laut" [Police Arrest Fisherman Pirate Accomplice at Sea], 15 June 2004, http://www.kompas.com (accessed 20 January 2005).

41. Apriadi Gunawan, "Fishermen shun Strait of Malacca for fear pirates", *Jakarta Post,* 10 May 2004, http://www.thejakartapost.com/Archives/ArchivesDet2.asp?FileID = 20040510.D02 (accessed 4 February 2005).

42. J. L. Anderson, "Piracy and World History: An Economic Perspective on Maritime Predation", *Journal of World History* 6, no. 2 (1995): 197.

43. Carolin Liss, "Maritime Piracy in Southeast Asia", *Southeast Asian Affairs 2003* (Singapore: Institute of Southeast Asian Studies, 2003), p. 61.

44. Eric Hobsbawm, *Bandits* (New York: Pantheon Books, 1981), pp. 13–14.

45. Ibid., p. 14.

46. For example, regarding an attack on the M/T *Tirta Niaga IV* which had

engine trouble in Indonesian waters on the Strait of Malacca: "she was surrounded by dozens of small boats from nearby communities. Dirt-poor villagers armed with long knives and clubs swarmed aboard her and captured the ship. It was apparently a spontaneous attack on a luckless vessel that had anchored off their *kampung*; it was too good to pass up, the riches had come to them (John Burnett, *Dangerous Waters: Modern Piracy and Terror on the High Seas* [New York: Dutton, 2002], p. 272). See also Michael Bociurkwic, "Pirate Says He Plunders to Feed His Family", *South China Morning Post*, 2 May 1993 in Liss, "Maritime Piracy", p. 62, detailing a Filipino pirate who claims to not like his job, but needs it to feed his family and to help take care of his neighbours and community, and Ian Williams, "Pirates of the Asiatic", *Channel 4 News Singapore*, 19 May 2005, http://www.channel4.com/news/index.html (accessed 4 June 2005).

47. "Tsunami may have washed away pirate problem", Reuters, 10 February 2005, http://www.stuff.co.nz/stuff/ (accessed 25 February 2005).

48. Although not specifically in reference to piracy the author describes several "security diminishing" aspects of the Riau, Johor, Singapore growth triangle. One of which was uneven distribution of economic benefit between the partners, particularly between Indonesian Riau and Singapore, where Singapore controls 3 per cent of the land but 90 per cent of the wealth; a statistic supporting this perception (Amitav Acharya, "Transnational Production and Security", *Contemporary Southeast Asia* 17, no. 2 [September 1995]: 182).

49. Greg Bankoff, *Crime, Society, and the State in the Nineteenth Century Philippines* (Manila: Ateneo de Manila University Press, 1996).

50. Although beyond the scope of this text, the difference in the role piracy plays in the community contemporarily, if any at all, would be an interesting study suggesting processes of cultural continuity and/or change relative to past practices.

51. Dian Murray, *Pirates of the South China Coast 1790–1810* (Stanford: Stanford University Press, 1987), p. 17.

52. Nikos Passas, "Globalization and Transnational Crime: Effects of Criminogenic Asymmetries", in *Combating Transnational Crime*, edited by P. Williams and D. Vlassis (London/Portland, OR: Frank Cass, 2001), p. 26.

53. Janice E. Thomson, *Mercenaries, Pirates, and Sovereigns* (Princeton: Princeton University Press, 1994), p. 19.

54. Previous to UNCLOS and the Archipelago Doctrine (both discussed in more detail later in this chapter) it was common practice to claim only 3 miles from the low tide mark, as compared to the 12 mile territorial sea and 200 mile EEZ now claimed by many littoral states.

55. FAO website at http://www.fao.org/fi/fcp/fcp.asp.

56. Ibid.

57. Sather, *Bajau Laut*, p. 87.

58. Ibid., p. 87.

59. Dupont, *East Asia Imperiled*, p. 142.

60. "TNI AL Usir 10,096 Kapal" [Indonesian Navy Chase 10,096 Ships], *Kompas*, 5 December 1997, p. 8, accessed in Tagliacozzo, *Secret Trades of the Straits*, p. 257.

61. Harold Crouch, *The Army and Politics in Indonesia* (Ithaca: Cornell University Press, 1978), p. 38.

62. Vagg, "Rough Seas?", p. 69.

63. Audrey Kahin, *Regional Dynamics of the Indonesian Revolution* (Honolulu: University of Hawaii Press, 1985), p. 127.

64. Johnstone, "The Sea Gypsies", pp. 47–48.

65. Bishen Bedi, "New Deal", *Malaysian Business*, 1 January 2002, Sec. Region, p. 64.

66. These have been largely economic refugees seeking better opportunities in Malaysia, but some political refugees from Aceh have been able to escape this way also, like the GAM leadership in exile in Sweden.

67. "Indonesia, Malaysia to Enhance Cooperation to Curb Smuggling", Xinhua News Agency, 28 August 2003. Also see "Malaysia launches massive operation to crack down on sea smuggling", Deutsche Presse-Agentur, 24 October 2004, sec. Miscellaneous.

68. Dr M. Isa Sulaiman, *Aceh Merdeka: Ideologi, Kepemimpinan dan Gerakan* [Free Aceh: Ideology, Leadership, and Political Movement] (Jakarta: Pustaka Al-Kaustar, 2000), p. 3.

69. Kate McGeown, "Aceh Rebels Blamed for Piracy", BBC News, 8 September 2003, http://news.bbc.co.uk/1/hi/world/asia-pacific/3090136.stm (accessed 14 March 2005).

70. Ibid.; see also Karen Teo, "New Piracy Attacks Put Spotlight on Indonesia", 18 August 2003, *Energy Intelligence Group, Inc.*, sec. Feature Stories; and Donald Urquhart, "Pirate Attacks Will Lead to Disaster in Malacca Straits", *Shipping Times*, 29 October 2003, sec. News.

71. Paul Dillon, "Did tsunamis ruin pirates of Sumatra?", *The Globe and Mail*, 25 January 2005, http://www.theglobeandmail.com/ (accessed 26 January 2005).

72. Kirsten E. Shulze, "The Struggle for an Independent Aceh", *Studies in Conflict and Terrorism* 26, no. 4 (2003): 254, 258.

73. "War Without End," *Economist* 367, no. 8322, 3 May 2003, p. 46.

74. Ronald J. May, "Muslim Mindanao: Four Years After the Peace", *Southeast Asian Affairs 2001* (Singapore: Institute of Southeast Asian Studies, 2001), p. 263, 13-page printout, *Academic Search Premier* online database, pp. 5–6.

75. Ferdinand Patinio, "CBCP Official Says Commission to Probe Sasa Wharf Bombing", *Manila Times*, 18 August 2003, sec. Top Stories, http://www.manilatimes.net/national/2003/aug/18/top_stories/20030818top9.html (accessed February 2004).

76. Michael Aung-Thwin, "Parochial Universalism, Democracy *Jihad*, and the Orientalist Image of Burma", *Pacific Affairs* 76, no. 4 (Winter 2001–02): 501.
77. Dupont, *East Asia Imperiled*, pp. 182–84. Of consideration to this text with its focus on Indonesia as a hot spot of piracy, an article from *Kompas* online quotes a high-ranking Indonesian naval commander stating that there are indications of international criminal syndicates in Indonesia being involved in piracy operations ("Sindikat Bajak Laut Internasional Kemungkinan Beraksi Di Indonesia" [International Pirate Syndicate Possibly Active in Indonesia], 18 September 2003, http://www.kompas.com (accessed 12 January 2005).
78. Incident related in Jayant Abhyankar, "Piracy and Ship Robbery: A Growing Menace", in *Combating Piracy and Ship Robbery: Charting the Future in Asia Pacific Waters*, edited by Hamzah Ahmad and Akira Ogawa (Tokyo: Okazaki Institute, 2001), p. 25. The *Alondra Rainbow* was carrying a cargo of aluminum ingots when it was hijacked just off Singapore. In large part, thanks to the efforts of the Piracy Reporting Centre in Kuala Lumpur, the *Alondra Rainbow*, renamed the *Mega Rama*, was found off the coast of India where it was finally arrested. The crew had been set adrift and recovered, but half the shipment of aluminum had already been offloaded.
79. "South Sea Piracy", *The Economist*, 18 December 1999, U.S. ed. The *Petro Ranger* was hijacked by "pirates", its cargo of fuel was offloaded to two other ships (value approximately $3 million). The ship was then arrested by Chinese officials on accusation of smuggling while the pirates were repatriated to Indonesia, and the owners had to pay a large "fee" to get the ship back.
80. Ibid. The *Tenyu* was carrying a cargo of aluminum ingots, like the *Alondra Rainbow*, when it disappeared in the South China Sea, only to turn up in a Chinese port on the Yangtze minus its cargo and crew.
81. P. Mukundun, "Piracy and Armed Robbery Against Ships Today", paper presented at the conference on "People and the Sea II: Conflicts, Threats and Opportunities", Amsterdam, 1 August 2003, p. 2.
82. Raja T. E. Simhan, "Wave of Piracy Hits Asia-Pacific Waters", *Businessline*, 17 November 2003, Islamabad, p. 1.
83. Beth Jinks, "Step up Security Measures, Harbour Craft Warned", *Shipping Times*, 14 January 2004, sec. News; "Piracy and Armed Robbery Against Ships Annual Report", 1 January – 31 December 2004, *Piracy Reporting Centre* (Kuala Lumpur: ICC International Maritime Bureau, 2004), p. 16.
84. "Chinese Military, Moro Insurgents Commit Piracy in South China Sea", *Businessworld*, 13 May 1999, p. 1.
85. Vagg, "Rough Seas?", p. 68.
86. See several articles in popular media as well as in scholarly reports, although both appear to be largely based on comments made by Eric Ellen, the director of the IMB, in regards to specific "piracy" cases: Alan Farnham,

"Pirates", *Fortune*, 15 July 1991, p. 112; Greg Torode, "Probe Into Stolen Ship Racket Leads to HK Firm", *South China Morning Post*, 25 July 1994, p. 4; "Report: Chinese May be Sanctioning Piracy", Associated Press, 9 March 1994; and more recently Matthew Flynn, "China Promises Crackdown as it Strives to Escape Image of a Safe Haven for Pirates", *Lloyd's List International*, 24 February 1999, p. 5; Abbot, and Renwick, "Pirates?", p. 14; and Michael Fabey, "Pirates Private and Public", *Traffic World* 256, no. 10, p. 26.

87. Michael Westlake, "But Is it Safe?: Sea and Air Accidents, Piracy Plague Cargo", *Far Eastern Economic Review* 155, no. 46, 19 November 1992, 45.

88. Flynn, "China Promises Crackdown".

89. Bertil Lintner, "Crime and Punishment?", *Far Eastern Economic Review* 165, no. 29 (25 July 2002), p. 46.

90. Ibid.

91. Greg Chaikin, "Maritime Regimes and Piracy in East Asia: Can Japan Climb Aboard?", paper presented at the conference on "People and the Sea II: Conflicts, Threats and Opportunities", Amsterdam, 1 August 2003, p. 5; Peter Chalk, "Contemporary Maritime Piracy in Southeast Asia", *Studies in Conflict and Terrorism* 21 (March 1997): 94.

92. The TNI was previously known as Angkatan Bersenjata Republik Indonesia or ABRI (The Republic of Indonesia Armed Forces), but in 1999 when the military was separated from police forces it was renamed TNI. See Damien Kingsbury, *Power Politics and the Indonesian Military* (London: Routledge Curzon, 2003), p. 248, fn. 1, Ch. 1. The other branches of the armed forces are the Angkatan Udara (Airforce), and Angkatan Darat (Army).

93. The TNI will be used as an inclusive reference to the military forces of Indonesia in general. When a specific branch of the armed forces is referenced their specific designation will be used, such as TNI AL. The separation between funding sources for the TNI as a whole and for each branch is unclear, so some ambiguity between the TNI and the TNI AL will be necessary.

94. David Jenkins, "The Military's Secret Cache", *Far Eastern Economic Review*, 8 February 1980, p. 70.

95. Kingsbury, *Power Politics*, p. 191.

96. Salim Osman, "Indonesian military seeks $10b budget", *Straits Times Interactive*, 26 February 2005, http://straitstimes.asia1.com.sg (accessed 26 February 2005).

97. See *A National Survey of Corruption in Indonesia: Final Report December 2001*, Partnership for Governance Reform in Indonesia (Jakarta, 2001), for a thorough look at corruption by government department and business sector in Indonesia.

98. "Those in Peril on the Sea", *Economist* 344, no. 8029, 9 August 1997, p. 40.

99. Ironically similar evidence has also been presented to implicate GAM in similar attacks.

100. Vagg, "Rough Seas?", p. 76.
101. Burnett, *Dangerous Waters*, p. 167.
102. Ibid.
103. See Chapter 1, pp. 7, 8, 9, for the text of Article 101.
104. Sam Bateman, "Maritime Transnational Violence: Problems of Control and Jurisdiction", paper presented for the seminar on "Transnational Crime" at the APCSS Biennial Conference in Honolulu, 16–18 July 2002.
105. United Nations General Assembly, Oceans and the Law of the Sea — Report of the Secretary General, 7 March 2002, U.N. Document A/57/57 para. 134, 26, cited in Bateman, "Maritime Transnational Violence".
106. For instance, see Tina Garmon, "International Law of the Sea: Reconciling the Law of 'Piracy' and Terrorism in the Wake of September 11th", *The Maritime Lawyer*, 27 March 2002; Timothy H. Goodman, "Leaving the Corsair's Name to Other Times", *Case Western Reserve Journal of International Law* (Winter 1999); Philip A. Buhler, "New Struggle with an Old Menace: Towards a Revised Definition of Maritime Piracy", *International Trade Law Journal* (Winter 1999); Sumihiko Kawamura, "Regional Cooperation Against Piracy and Armed Robbery", in *Combating "Piracy" and Ship Robbery*, edited by Ahmad and Ogawa; and Jay L. Batongbacal, "Trends in Anti-Piracy Cooperation in the ASEAN Region", in *Combating "Piracy" and Ship Robbery*, edited by Ahmad and Ogawa; among many others.
107. John Mo, "Options to Combat Maritime Piracy in Southeast Asia", *Ocean Development & International Law* 33, no. 3–4 (2002): 348.
108. See Australian Maritime Safety Authority, http://imo.amsa.gov.au/public/parties/sua88.html (accessed 4 June 2005); and "S'pore accedes to anti-maritime terror pact", *Straits Times*, 4 February 2004, sec. Singapore.
109. Batongbacal, "Trends in Anti-Piracy Cooperation", p 126.
110. Ibid., p. 125.
111. SUA, Article 10, subsec. 1.
112. Hamzah B. Ahmad, "Piracy and Ship Robbery: An Introduction", in *Combating "Piracy" and Ship Robbery*, edited by Ahmad and Ogawa, p. 7.
113. Dino Patti Djalal, *The Geopolitics of Indonesia's Maritime Territorial Policy* (Jakarta: Centre for Strategic and International Studies, 1996), p. 121. This attitude stems from the last forty years where Indonesia has developed the concept of *Wawasan Nusantara*, drawn in large part from the Archipelago Doctrine, which incorporates the idea of the unity of the Indonesian Archipelago as a fundamental aspect of national identity, economic development, and strategic outlook. This concept formed in large part due to strategic and symbolic considerations, in reaction to Dutch and Japanese colonial history as well as intervention by other foreign powers, such as the United States in clandestine CIA support of insurrections in 1957, British support of Dutch attempts to retake Indonesia after World War II, and even perceived Chinese support of the Indonesian Communist Party prior to 1965. Thus any attempt perceived to have the potential to compromise any

aspect of Indonesia's control of its maritime territory, particularly by any of these countries, is taken as an assault on Indonesian sovereignty and identity. This includes any perceived "internationalization", or giving some control over these waterways to other countries or international organizations.

114. Zou Keyuan, "Enforcing the Law of Piracy in the South China Sea", *Journal of Maritime Law & Commerce* (January 2000): 7.

115. Walden Bello, "The Insecurity of Asia's Financial Crisis", *Peace Review* 11, no. 3 (September 1999): 393–99.

116. "Piracy Resurgence", p. 11.

117. "Malaysia, Thailand to Start Border Patrols", *Asian Wall Street Journal*, 12 January 2004.

118. "Japan to Send Patrol Vessel to Singapore for Anti-Piracy", *Japan Economic Newswire*, 19 November 2003, sec. International News.

119. Vagg, "Rough Seas?", p. 77.

120. Ibid.

121. ASEAN Secretariat, http://www.aseansec.org/home.htm (accessed 16 March 2005); "Manila Declaration on the Prevention and Control of Transnational Crime", February 1998, http://www.aseansec.org/home.htm (accessed 13 January 2005); "Joint Communiqué The First ASEAN Plus Three Ministerial Meeting on Transnational Crime (AMMTC + 3)", Bangkok, January 2004, http://www.aseansec.org/home.htm (accessed 13 January 2005); "Joint Communiqué of the Second ASEAN Ministerial Meeting on Transnational Crime", January 2004, http://www.aseansec.org/home.htm (accessed 13 January 2005); "Memorandum of Understanding Between the Governments of the Member Countries of the Association of Southeast Asian Nations (ASEAN) and the Government of the People's Republic of China on Cooperation in the Field of Non-traditional Security Issues", November 2002, http://www.aseansec.org/home.htm (accessed 13 January 2005), "Work Program to Implement the ASEAN Plan of Action to Combat Transnational Crime", sect. 3-3.6, http://www.aseansec.org/home.htm (accessed 13 January 2005),.

122. Singapore has recently announced that it will begin boarding and escorting "sensitive" ships through its territorial waters in order to protect ships deemed sensitive to terrorist attack, which could also protect vulnerable ships against piracy as well. ("Singapore navy to escort commercial ships", Reuters, 28 February 2005, http://www.arabtimesonline.com/arabtimes/ breaking news, accessed 1 March 2005). The cost and practicability for larger maritime nations would be debatable however.

123. Djalal, *Geopolitics of Indonesia's Maritime Territorial Policy*, p. 121.

124. Barret Bingley, "U.S. interests in Malacca Straits", *Jakarta Post*, 17 July 2004, http://www.thejakartapost.com/Archives/ArchivesDet2.asp? FileID = 20040707.E03 (accessed 14 January 2005).

125. Tiarma Siboro, "More Countries to Patrol Malacca Strait", *Jakarta Post*,

7 August 2004, http://www.thejakartapost.com/Archives/ArchivesDet2.asp? FileID = 20040807.B01 (accessed 4 February 2005).

126. Dillion, "Did tsunamis ruin pirates of Sumatra?".

127. "Piracy and Armed Robbery Against Ships Annual Report", 2004, p. 5.

128. Illegal fishing is an important priority for Indonesia, competing for resources that could potentially be given to piracy, but it does not have much historical significance and so was left as a footnote only. See the following for discussion of illegal fishing itself, and its effects on piracy: Fegan, "Plundering the Sea", p. 1 of 5; M. J. Peterson, "An Historical Perspective on the Incidents of Piracy", in *Piracy at Sea*, edited by Eric Ellen (Paris: International Chamber of Commerce, International Maritime Bureau, 1989), p. 49; see also Irwan Siregar et al., "Aman Berkat Praktik Ali Baba" [It is Peaceful because of the Practice of Ali Baba], *Gamma* 2, no. 5: 74–75; "DKP Bertekad Terus Berantas Pencurian Ikan" [Ministry of Maritime Affairs and Fisheries Fight Illegal Fishing], *Republika online*, 31 January 2005, http://www.republika.co.id/koran_detail.asp?id = 185768&kat_id = 4 (accessed 2 February 2005); "Indonesia's Losses from Foreign Fish Poachers Down 50 Pct", *Asia Pulse*, 24 September 2003, sec. Northern Regional Territory; "Indonesia says illegal fishing crackdown is successful", ABC Radio Australia, 2 January 2004 http://www.eurocbc.org/ indonesian_sinking_policy_curbs_illegal_fishing_02jan2004page1390.html (accessed 3 February 2005).

129. As of 2003 Indonesia had approximately 117 ships (2 submarines, 14 warships, 57 patrol boats, and 44 support vessels/supply and transport ships) to patrol the entirety of their archipelagic waters, of which only 35 per cent were at sea ("Navy to buy two submarines", *Jakarta Post*, 19 September 2003, sec. Front page; "Pirates of the Malacca Straits on a roll", Deutsche Presse-Agentur, 28 September 2003, sec. Miscellaneous.) Furthermore, many *kabupaten* (administrative unit below a province) that have extensive maritime territory do not have any patrol craft at all ("Selat Sunda Rawan Perompakan" [Southern Sunda Disturbed by Piracy], *Kompas*, 9 October 2003, sec. Nusantara http://www.kompas.com/kompas-cetak/ 0310/09/daerah/613872.htm) (accessed 27 March 2004).

130. Interpol, http://www.interpol.int/Public/Statistics/ICS/downloadList.asp (accessed 27 March 2004).

131. Even factoring in underreporting of piracy incidents, if they are statistically compared to land-based criminal activity, piracy is insignificant.

132. Tagliacozzo, *Secret Trades of the Straits*, p. 377.

133. Robert Stuart, *In Search of Pirates: A Modern-Day Odyssey* (Edinburgh: Mainstream, 2002), p. 195.

134. Peter Chalk, *Non-Military Security and Global Order* (London: Macmillan Press, 2000), p. 8.

135. Jeffery Boutwell and Micheal Klare, "Small Arms and Light Weapons:

Controlling the Real Instruments of War", *Arms Control Today* 28 (August/ September 1998): 16.

136. Chalk, *Non-Military Security*, pp. 10–12.

137. "Piracy Resurgence", p. 11.

138. Burnett, *Dangerous Waters*, pp. 6, 176.

139. Ibid., p. 167.

140. Llyods Registry, http://www.lr.org/market_sector/marine/maritime-security/faqs.htm (accessed 27 March 2004).

141. See accounts from non-fiction novels such as Burnett's *Dangerous Waters* and Rob Stuart's *In Search of Pirates*, as well as incidents reported in the media such as Keith Bradsher, "Warnings From Al Qaeda Stir Fear That Terrorists May Attack Oil Tankers", *New York Times*, 12 December 2002, Sec. A.

142. Wooden boats are often hard to spot on radar (Bradsher, "Warnings From Al Qaeda") unless of a very sophisticated variety, and waves can cause "static" that can mask relatively small boats.

143. Burnett, *Dangerous Waters*, p. 164.

144. Chalk, *Non-Military Security*, p. 60.

145. International Maritime Bureau-Piracy Reporting Center, http://www.iccwbo.org/ccs/menu_imb_piracy.asp (accessed 27 March 2004).

146. These kinds of security features will be further discussed with other information technology later in the chapter.

147. Batongbacal, "Trends in Anti-Piracy Cooperation", p. 28.

148. Ibid., p. 109; Chalk, "Contemporary Maritime Piracy", 97.

149. Several articles appearing in *Tajuk*, vol. 3, issue 15 (15–29 September 2000), pp. 14–23, 36–38, dealt with the issue of false importers, smuggling, and corruptible port officials implicating Indonesian Customs, suggesting the culpability of these officials.

150. In 2004 the IMB recorded 148 hostages taken in reported piracy incidents, making the total number of hostages for 2000–2004 to be 1,110, and since 1993 there have been 2,705. Although it is unclear if in the years before 2004 the numbers also include kidnap/ransom victims. Either way the taking of hostages has been significant.

151. Dupont, *East Asia Imperiled*, p. 191.

152. David Osler, "Global Piracy Bill", *Lloyd's List International*, 11 December 2002, p. 1.

153. Burnett, *Dangerous Waters*, p. 265; Bradsher, "Warnings From Al Qaeda".

154. Ken Cottrill, "Modern Marauders", *Popular Mechanics* 174, no. 12 (December 1997): 78–79.

155. Dupont, *East Asia Imperiled*, pp. 174, 176; Passas, "Globalization and Transnational Crime", pp. 31–32.

156. Passas, "Globalization and Transnational Crime", pp. 30, 31.

157. Burnett, *Dangerous Waters*, p. 264. This account involving pirates posing as

fishermen is anecdotal, but a convincing account nonetheless and very suggestive of potential tactics for pirates.

158. A pirate posed as a fishing vessel and requested fuel and/or food from another fisherman, but upon approach the pirate robbed the would-be helper. "Takut Perompak, Nelayan Tak Melaut" [Afraid of Piracy Fishermen Don't Go to Sea], *Kompas*, 14 December 2004, http://kompas.com (accessed 13 Janaury 2005).

159. Stuart, *In Search of Pirates*, p. 195. It is also interesting to note that these surprise tactics are also not always used, as in several cases involving tankers, barges, and even fishermen the targets were brought to a halt by openly firing on the boat ("Piracy and Armed Robbery Against Ships Annual Report", 2003, p. 16).

160. James Francis Warren, *Iranun and Balangingi: Globalization, Maritime Raiding and the Birth of Ethnicity* (Quezon City: New Day Publishers, 2002), p. 174.

161. Ibid., pp. 346–48.

162. Ibid., p. 177.

4

Conclusions and A Way Forward

Maritime piracy has a long, interesting, and involved history in the region, and the continuity of the roots of historical and contemporary piracy highlight the endemic nature of piracy in the region. This chapter will summarize and analyse continuities between historical and contemporary piracy already mentioned earlier, highlighting several structural underpinnings of piracy that provide the motivation and opportunity for piracy to emerge. This suggests an overall approach to addressing the roots of contemporary maritime piracy that emphasizes structural development and increased operational capacities of the littoral states. Of particular concern is Indonesia, which is responsible for securing an enormous maritime territory but is hampered by a variety of domestic and international issues.

A WAY FORWARD

- Contemporary maritime piracy has its roots in the maritime socio-cultural matrix of the region that makes piracy a thinkable option. Weak state development, unable to cope with rapid economic and societal changes, which cannot effectively provide access to or distribute economic benefits, or effectively include maritime-oriented peoples in a national identity, has created a large group of marginalized maritime-oriented peoples facing endemic poverty, making piracy increasingly thinkable.
- Gaps in the state's political hegemony stemming from the state's inability to control the means of its own legitimacy hamper the state's ability to address piracy, making piracy more practicable.
- Lack of state control over the technical means of carrying out piracy, particularly the state's inability to regulate access to and to develop their own intelligence to counter the complimentary technology of pirates, and the lack of vessels, further makes piracy possible.

As Batongbacal has succinctly put it, "The long-term goal should be not only to suppress piracy and sea robbery when it takes place, but to create a regional environment that inherently prevents piracy and sea robbery from even being considered by anyone."[1] The deep roots of piracy in maritime Southeast Asia makes this goal overly ambitious, but its emphasis on prevention and long-term solutions mirrors the approach that has been suggested throughout this text. To this end, policy should have two main thrusts — developing policing and operational maritime security capacities, and structural development, i.e. economic and political development. Both of these are important in addressing current regional states' inabilities to exercise control and regulate maritime peoples, secure gaps in the political hegemony, and control the tactical means of piracy.

This chapter will explore policy directions based on the above analysis of contemporary piracy through historical context, first looking at the theme of international co-operation primarily as a source for funding and training, focusing on developing local capacities. It will then discuss various aspects of "policing", emphasizing increasing domestic operational capacities. The importance of structural development in changing the environment from which piracy has emerged by addressing the roots of contemporary piracy directly will be looked at next. Following this will be a discussion on the importance of increasing the base of primary research on piracy, through both statistical and social science-based quantitative and qualitative methods. From this information the issues surrounding piracy in Southeast Asia can be better contextualized, developing approaches to understanding piracy, facilitating tailoring policy, and directing resources on a regional and sub-regional scale.

INTERNATIONAL CO-OPERATION

The transnational nature of piracy has become the focus of much of the security dialogue on the subject. Indeed the mobility and fluidity with which pirates operate between national borders would suggest a multilateral co-operative approach in addressing the issue. This is problematic however, as discussed earlier, particularly in the Singapore and Malacca Straits, as the issue of internationalization of security raises the spectre of regional, and/or worse, extra-regional interference in the sovereignty of the littoral states. The recent Malsindo patrols, as well as past co-operative patrols in the Straits region, suggest that Indonesia and

Malaysia are willing to share responsibility of security in this region to a point. The point where these countries can enter each other's territorial waters for routine patrolling, or even in hot pursuit of pirates, has not been reached yet, and will not be likely in the near future. With regard to extra-regional powers participating in patrols, both Indonesia and Malaysia have been very upfront in their unwillingness to entertain this possibility, particularly with Japan and the United States. While understandable, this does problematize the legitimate concerns of extra-regional powers in the ability of the littoral states to provide security in the region, but only if their involvement entails direct participation of their security forces. While pressure from extra-regional powers, through such measures as the Regional Maritime Security Initiative (RMSI), have pressured littoral states to publicly acknowledge the problem and take at least some steps towards addressing it, this pressure has done nothing to change the domestic conditions that are the source of the problem.

Regional security co-operation in this sense appears to be a way of extra-regional and regional states wagging their fingers at the perceived weak links in the regional security chain, but little else. International co-operation has focused on solutions that will only delay the next outbreak of piracy until conditions are again ripe. While joint co-operation is ultimately necessary to address transnational security issues like piracy, the first priority must be to establish domestic security regimes and capabilities that address the issue. If states like Indonesia and the Philippines are not able to secure their own waters, control the development of independent loci of power within their states, and offer their people a way out of poverty, transnational co-operation will be problematic. Regional security is being compromised from within these states, so that patrols with their neighbours on the outside of their borders are of little use in addressing where and how these security problems are developing.

One of the main roles of international co-operation should be to provide funding and training to develop national operational security capacities, and for structural development. International co-operation in addressing piracy needs to focus on the roots of contemporary maritime piracy, i.e. the domestic issues in Indonesia and other states that have pushed maritime-oriented peoples towards piracy, and compromised the state's ability to check these trends. Piracy in the nineteenth century was brought under control when the colonial powers had settled their own domestic issues and could thereby extend their economic and political control. Moreover, it was often their ambiguous lack of commitment to the region resulting from the bottom line of their financial ledgers, or the genuine inability to provide the needed security, that allowed for raiding and piracy to run rampant through much of the latter eighteenth and nineteenth centuries. When it was brought under control, they had taken effective steps to consolidate their political hegemony in the region, which removed the spaces where piracy/raiding could operate. International and multilateral efforts to address piracy in the region need to focus on helping to build national security, then, as with the European powers in the nineteenth century, co-operation will become more likely and more effective.

Indonesia and the rest of ASEAN have given tacit approval to this approach as suggested by their assent to steps addressing sea piracy, which includes the role of extra-regional co-operation in technical assistance and funding.[2] This form of international co-operation is less threatening than military or security co-operation and will more effectively address the root causes of piracy. International shipping companies could also play a role in supporting the development of impoverished regions they transit, as it would be in their interest to appear more as a friendly face with a helping hand, and less as just a "rich passer-by".[3] Without the willing and committed co-operation of regional states like Indonesia, which will only be possible once their more immediate domestic issues have been addressed, international efforts to address piracy will be difficult.

POLICING

A first step should focus on developing intelligence networks in order to use available resources more efficiently, and direct where resources can be most effectively applied. State agencies need to find out who the pirates are, where they are operating from, how their intelligence networks function, what their planned targets are, as well as tracking the organization and operations of pirates across the region. Piracy is not just a sea-borne menace, as with historical piracy, but it radiates out from bases and operational centres. The raiding and piracy of the nineteenth century was brought under control as their bases were eliminated, and so policing efforts also need to deal with these hubs, using their intelligence networks to locate, infiltrate and arrest gangs. As long as there are safe havens to operate from, patrols and surveillance will only be a casual deterrent to pirates. Developing intelligence networks will allow them to strike at their weakest, most sedentary points — their home bases.

This also entails establishing routine communication and intelligence sharing with counterparts in foreign countries, in order to organize operations across the region, or at least allow each state to keep tabs on piracy operations that routinely cross national borders. Much of this intelligence is likely already available, but through a wilful breakdown in the intelligence by security forces and port officials co-opted by corruption, or simply hamstringed by financial problems, they lack the will and/or ability to follow up on it. Steps should also be taken to control what intelligence is available to pirates both by addressing corruption in security forces and port authorities, and by making shipping information more secure. Shipping companies and port authorities need to better filter what employees they hire and who has access to vital information such as the cargo manifest and shipping route.

States also need to increase their operational capacities by simply having sufficient quantity and quality of vessels to be able to patrol vital areas of their vast maritime territories, and if need be to pursue pirates. As steam power did for colonial powers, an increase in operational capacities would reduce the possible scope of their attacks, reduce the vulnerability of targets, and hopefully restrict their ability to escape and hide. Having more vessels available to patrol, secure, and regulate use of their borders, and respond to incidents will as much as possible eliminate the "safe" spaces that pirates operate in, reducing their tactical advantage. The quicker security forces can react to an incident, the narrower the advantage pirates have. A greater security presence would also help deter opportunist pirates by limiting their opportunities and increasing their risks.

In terms of weapons, little can be done to remove weapons such as knives or clubs from pirates, and there is little point in trying to "out-gun" pirates, because direct conflict with security forces is typically what they try to avoid. What needs to be done is to tighten the control and sale of firearms, severely restricting access to these weapons, and prevent them from falling into the hands of the pirates in the first place. Increased operational capacities can also help address this issue by restricting smuggling networks, which in turn will help contain illegal markets that provide access to light arms used by some pirates, and by secessionist movements alike. Controlling smuggling would also help regulate markets willing to deal in pirated goods.

As was the case with the Dutch, Spanish, and to some degree the British in the nineteenth century, a lack of suitable patrol craft drastically limit the scope of security that can be provided. Currently Indonesia has an extremely limited maritime security capacity, most of which is part of their navy. This is problematic as navies tend to focus budgets on purchasing large ships meant for national-level defence, such as submarines, frigates, and missile boats, whereas what is most needed for anti-piracy efforts are small, fast patrol vessels able to outrun pirate speed boats, and pursue them into shallow coastal waters.[4] Additionally, surveillance aircraft would also be an important asset in covering the vast maritime spaces, but cost is a limiting factor.[5] To address this international funds, training, and materials should be provided for these states to develop national coast guards,[6] or equivalent civil security forces, separate from military structures. The former should be focused on addressing larger-scale conflicts, and not having to engage in police functions. In the long run coast guards would also help facilitate regional co-operation as they are not as threatening to sovereignty as are national militaries. Currently Japan is one of the very few states outside the region engaged in such capacity-building, and yet they are certainly not alone in the benefits they derive from the strategic waters of Southeast Asia.

Once intelligence networks and more anti-piracy vessels have helped contain and arrest pirates there needs to be a comprehensive legal regime in order to deal with them. This includes having laws to prosecute pirates, taking into account the diversity of modern piracy, as well as having appropriate extradition and co-operative legal procedures. The frequency with which pirates operate across borders suggests that when more pirates are being arrested this will become an important issue. The model national law created by the Comite Maritime International forms a comprehensive approach to addressing maritime violence,[7] maintaining the United Nations Convention on the Law of the Sea (UNCLOS) Article 101 definition of piracy and making room for any national statues on the topic, but putting everything else under "Maritime Violence". This law has the benefit of covering all maritime violence regardless of distinctions of political or private gain motives, thus putting jurisdiction and legal redressment fully in the hands of the state rather than dictated by potentially controversial international statutes.

STRUCTURAL DEVELOPMENT

Essentially the maritime-oriented lifestyle is at the heart of piracy, and what of this can be changed without seriously transgressing the social contract between the state and its people needs to be addressed. The way to do this is by developing policy that is specifically aimed at positively changing this lifestyle. Accordingly economic and political development targeted towards solving these issues will address these roots of piracy.

Economic development targeted towards coastal regions and maritime peoples where piracy is a problem, such as Riau, Aceh, and the Sulu Archipelago, is an important and obvious place to start. International funds should be directed at encouraging sustainable economic development and opportunities in littoral regions,[8] with the goal of alleviating the most extreme and pervasive poverty among maritime populations, and widening the buffer zone between survival and abject poverty, thus seeking to abrogate motivations for turning to piracy. Furthermore, access to a steady income and the nature of the consumer world we live in will draw people into having a stake in the legitimate economic processes of the state. Part of this effort should be directed at including marginalized maritime populations in the identity of the state, thereby developing genuine loyalty and binding them to legitimate power structures. Indeed, the state needs to find a way to respectfully and positively include maritime peoples in the national identity, without levelling local identities. This will address the socio-cultural matrix that makes piracy still thinkable in the region by drawing people out of traditional conceptions of broad-based survival strategy, both in terms of historical continuity of cultural norms that may have escaped the last 150 years of modern state building, and in terms of the chronic subsistence-level survival and endemic poverty of many maritime-oriented peoples. In this way, economic development will be able to directly address the majority of piracy in the region — low-end ad hoc piracy, which threatens the lives and livelihoods of local fishermen and traders.

Economic development is not a panacea for piracy in itself, as these measures would not directly address the motivations for high-end organized piracy that hijack and dispose of entire ships, which can net millions of dollars. The motivation for these attacks is beyond what general economic development can directly address, but such incidents are also by far the minority. Economic development could, however, help dry up the large potential labour pool of pirates from which these organizations are likely recruiting. Additionally, reducing the number of recruits now could in the future reduce the number of experienced, hardened pirates that are responsible for brutal attacks, like that involving the *Tenyu*. A steady, legitimate income could make the difference to many people for whom piracy is a thinkable option.

Political development is also necessary to facilitate economic development and to address gaps in the state political hegemony. One of the first priorities must be settling the instability stemming from separatist movements in regions such as Mindanao and Aceh. The instability resulting from these movements is a serious drain on security resources, has created lawless zones beyond state control, and draws firearms and other weapons, which pirates also use, into the region. The instability also prevents people there from establishing a stable life, economically or otherwise, making them vulnerable to societal pressures and economic instability that can push them towards piracy.

Also of concern are issues surrounding the patronage of piracy and corruption within the state. Corruption is invasive and pervasive, and once settled into the routines of the state as it is in Indonesia, it is difficult to dislodge as the mechanisms for doing so are part of the corrupt structure.[9] However, to address the roots of contemporary piracy this issue needs to be taken into hand. If corruption can be brought under control in the state, it will cut off a large part of the influence from organized crime and other criminal elements, even down to small gangs of pirates that potentially take advantage of corrupt local regulatory and security officials. Of course, steps also need to be taken to address criminal syndicates that provide the resources and organization to steal and dispose of entire ships and their crews, but these operations will become much more difficult if they do not have access to the state.

Another aspect of political development important to consider is the organization and co-operation of state offices charged with maritime security. As an example, in Indonesia maritime security is shared among numerous departments and security forces, including naval forces, police, the Department of Marine Affairs and Fisheries (Departmen Kelautan dan Perikanan), and numerous others that all have a say in how Indonesia prioritizes and organizes maritime security. In Malaysia a similar situation had developed. However, the government is in the process of consolidating maritime security under one agency, the Malaysian Maritime Security Agency (MMEA), which should provide greater organization and co-operation among Malaysia's various maritime concerns. If successful, the MMEA could provide an example for other regional states to follow in organizing their maritime security forces. Consolidation of maritime security forces would also likely facilitate co-operation, both in terms of domestic forces, and also in terms of international security forces.

The funds necessary for these steps are beyond the means of nations like Indonesia, hard hit by the Asian economic crisis and the resulting political turmoil. This is where international co-operation can be of great use, and in a largely non-threatening manner, although international aid rarely comes without strings attached. Funding and training for the development of maritime security capacities should at least in part come from those that benefit from a stable security environment, i.e. concerned regional and extra-regional states, as well as private shipping companies.

INFORMATION GATHERING

Policies addressing piracy, both in terms of policing and structural development, need to be contextualized to Southeast Asia, and more specifically to states, regions, and sub-regions that make up Southeast Asia which are affected by piracy. In order to do this policy-makers and analysts need a better understanding of the nature of piracy in the region, which can be accomplished by greatly expanding the body of primary information available to academics and analysts. This includes more thoroughly compiling statistical data on incidents of piracy, as well as expanding academic research on the subject.

The statistics and incident reports now compiled by the International Maritime Bureau (IMB) are of use in assessing piracy, but they also have substantial shortcomings. The IMB is performing a true service by compiling incident reports from around the world. However, the statistics are not without criticism. Shipping companies have complained that by using such an inclusive definition, piracy numbers may be inflated, damaging their reputations and increasing insurance rates,[10] a criticism that would also likely be seconded by the littoral nations of Southeast Asia that are continually shown as hotspots of piracy by the IMB Piracy Reporting Centre (IMB-PRC). However, the IMB-PRC suggests that their definition has the benefit of more accurately reflecting the complex reality that shipowners and their crews face when they ply the waters of Southeast Asia. This particular way of defining and understanding piracy would not be much of an issue, except for the importance that IMB-PRC statistics have assumed over the last fifteen years. Aside from issues directly pertaining to how the IMB-PRC has chosen to define piracy, and thus determine what information they include, there are also several issues stemming from the IMB-PRC that are not directly of their making.

Under-reporting of incidents of piracy is a major issue, due to several reasons, such as the potential costs of delays in shipping and raises in insurance.[11] Additionally, many incidents involving fishermen or other local commercial traffic, despite their prevalence, with at least fifteen Indonesian fishing vessels attacked between January and May 2004,[12] are likely not reported to the IMB-PRC,[13] because they may not ever be reported to local authorities and there is no guarantee that local authorities would report them to the IMB-PRC. Furthermore, a possible violence bias in reported incidents may also skew the picture of piracy being presented, as a disproportionate number of attacks that require hospitalization may be reported to the authorities.[14] Furthermore, the IMB is a private organization drawing its income largely from international commercial shipping groups and insurance agencies, and therefore it must ultimately frame its ideas of piracy keeping its patrons in mind. This means that pirate attacks against local shipping, which is hard to gather information about in the first place, is not of as much interest to the funding sources of the PRC despite its probable majority of incidents. These statistical irregularities have important implications as the IMB-PRC statistics are widely used.

The ubiquity of IMB-PRC statistics has unintentionally led to a veritable one-sided definitional and informational regime in piracy literature, which is potentially problematic for several reasons. One reason is because discussions and policy are being based on one source of incomplete data and statistics. A recent example of the importance that IMB statistics have taken on is an article in *The Australian*. The article reports that navy chief Rear Admiral Chris Ritche, citing IMB statistics describing increasing incidents of piracy, has outlined how Australian warships will play a greater role in countering threats (such as piracy) to shipping.[15] Furthermore, while it may be lending more weight to policy literature than it owes, much of the contemporary piracy literature used for this text have cited IMB-PRC statistics, which has an impact on the issue as it is eventually addressed in track one and two dialogues. The ubiquitous use of IMB-PRC data is also problematic because the definition of piracy used to gather this data is not in agreement with legal definitions, although it has potential implications for legal enforcement as it intersects and interacts with security policy.

Essentially this is a problem of what data is available and how it is being used, and does not negate all beneficial use of their information. The nature of the statistics needs to be kept in mind when using them for analysis, as it has been for this book. These issues surrounding IMB-PRC statistics also points to a continuing situation where there is a dearth of primary data on piracy. Efforts should be made to expand the scope of primary information on piracy available for analysis, including incorporating more humanities and social science-based research, as well as expanding efforts at gathering, and/or starting new sources of statistics. Part of this problem is the simple fact that in modern times any good pirate will be an unknown pirate, because it is a crime carrying often harsh punishments,[16] not something to be glorified. This creates a dearth of information as agents of piracy seek anonymity, and thus their motivations and stories are hidden.

To address this, more funding should be made available for data collection, either under the control of the IMB, or through the formation of an ASEAN or International Maritime Organization (IMO) regional centre. An ASEAN-based effort may find regional co-operation easier, but a United Nations-funded centre through the IMO would have better access to worldwide statistics. One way to organize the compilation of information could be through Interpol, which has better access to national information, and could provide direct access to the information for all state security forces involved with Interpol. A more thorough compilation of incidents of maritime violence, along the definitional lines of the IMB, would better contextualize regional hotspots of piracy, like Southeast Asia, in comparison to other parts of the world,[17] and would help in further assessing what the threat of piracy really is.

Future research on piracy needs to follow two key avenues: first, piracy should be placed within the broader context of other transnational and non-traditional threats facing the maritime regions of Southeast Asia such as smuggling, illegal fishing, and environmental degradation; and second, research needs to emphasize primary data collection at the local level. Piracy itself is not an issue of supreme urgency, as suggested by the above discussions, in the sense that it does not threaten immediate state collapse. However, it is part of a suite of security issues that cross national boundaries, openly utilizing the contested boundaries of Southeast Asia to their benefit, and which threatens the quality of life for significant portions of the population. Moreover, these security threats all tend to emerge from unstable or poorly regulated socio-political-cultural environments, largely due to widespread economic and political dysfunction.

Understandings of piracy also need to go beyond the numbers and types of incidents, and need to include broadening pirate research into the social sciences like anthropology, sociology, geography, and into multidisciplinary approaches such as those cultivated through regional studies programmes. Understanding the political economy, social geography, and societal and cultural roles of piracy would help analysts tailor policy on more specific terms than broad regional security approaches. In order to better understand piracy and other non-traditional security threats, and provide concrete suggestions of what the nature of the threats are and how to address them, the local context needs to be researched. Understanding how the threat is perceived and what are enabling factors on a micro-scale, substantiated through case studies, would provide valuable insight into piracy and other non-traditional security issues. Case studies involving pirates, possibly based on interviews with prisoners, their families and communities would be particularly interesting and revealing about the motivation for and operations of piracy in the region. To this end an area of research that needs to be developed is local scholarship on contemporary piracy, both for the perspective of people from the region, and because the sensitive nature of the subject may be more approachable through local scholars rather than foreigners.

CONCLUSIONS

This text has emphasized the utility of using history in trying to address the roots of contemporary maritime piracy in Southeast Asia, and from this approach it has been shown that the roots of contemporary piracy lay in the modern socio-cultural-political environment of maritime Southeast Asia. This historical context is predominantly from the recent colonial past reaching to the first arrival of Europeans in the sixteenth century, but also tangibly stretches into the prehistory of the region, involving conceptions of power, social organization, and trade dynamics that contributed to early state development in maritime Southeast Asia. Before Western conceptions of legalistic states eclipsed local state structures based on charismatic leadership, the manifold phenomena encased in the word "piracy" was an intrinsic element of the socio-cultural-political matrix. Today the vestiges or guises of these historical conceptions of power still permeate power dynamics in the region, but piracy does not hold the same status that it once did. However, the continued prevalence of maritime-oriented peoples and the continuities linking these peoples with their past, culturally and materially, combined with the cyclic underpinnings of piracy based on prevailing economic and political circumstances, has ensured that piracy, while no longer intrinsic, is still endemic to the region.

The threat posed by piracy in the waters of Southeast Asia is very real, particularly in its daily threat to local traffic, but also to international shipping. However, when contextualized in Southeast Asia as one of a number of regional security issues its direct threat to life and commerce is relatively low, but significant because of the strategic region where it is active, and because of potential long-term economic implications, as trade may seek alternative routes around piracy hotspots. Piracy is a low-level security threat in a highly strategic area, but emblematic of broader issues of weak state control over economic and political circumstances, epitomized by the challenges to maritime security facing Indonesia. Piracy as a security threat emerges from these circumstances and therefore needs to be contextualized within these broader problems. What this means for policy addressing piracy in Southeast Asia is that no amount of security or structural change in the near future will totally eliminate piracy, similar to the situation at the end of the nineteenth century. The most that can be hoped for, and should be the goal of policy addressing the issue, is a comprehensive, progressive economic and political agenda that will change the socially and economically marginal lifestyles of many maritime-oriented peoples in the region, and provide local capabilities for better policing these vast sea spaces. These sea spaces are now under the sovereignty of the littoral states of Southeast Asia, thereby placing these states under obligation to provide security upon threat to their legitimacy in the eyes of their people and the international community.

The outlook and feasibility of the policy directions outlined in this text, emphasizing a comprehensive and progressive economic and political agenda to address the roots of contemporary piracy, are mixed. As mentioned earlier there seems to be widespread support nationally, regionally and beyond, for stepping up policing efforts in the vital choke points of the region, but support for developing the national capabilities of providing internal security seems to be lacking. It is possible that recent re-establishment of U.S.–Indonesian military ties combined with limited support from other extra-regional security partners like Japan, may begin to address this. The real problem is generating international support for security policies that address the more structural elements of piracy, the poverty and marginal lifestyles, which to all appearances is nowhere on the radar right now. Disappointingly, the whole thrust of this book stemming from analysis of the historical context of piracy has been that these are the very issues that most need to be tackled if piracy is to be addressed in the long term.

It is possible that the devastation of the 26 December 2004 tsunami and the massive, international, multilateral aid effort in Aceh could provide evidence for the efficacy of this structural approach to maritime security policy. When the international community withdraws, and/if the aid money continues to flow, it may be seen what effect the rebuilding of huge coastal regions can do to affect piracy in the long term. Surely some piracy will return, as is already the case with several reported incidents,[18] but on what scale and by who is yet to be seen. Predominantly local piracy, composed largely of local thugs and gangs from regional impoverished maritime-oriented peoples, may have greater difficulty restarting their operations, due to the destruction of pirate vessels and other assets, including the deaths of the pirates themselves, and limited access to capital for new assets. However, more organized elements may resurface relatively quickly due to greater access to capital. A recent spate of attacks and kidnappings in the northern end of the Malacca Strait would seem to support this supposition.[19]

Piracy in its threat to human life and to safe navigation is an immediate concern that policy-makers need to address, and to some degree with limited success this is being done as regional patrols are organized, and piracy is consistently on the agenda of regional security dialogues. However, if the disparities between the domestic security capacities, and more importantly, the asymmetries between economic and political development of the littoral states in Southeast Asia are not addressed, then the continued prevalence of piracy will be assured. It is not enough to cut at the tops and hope that the weed will not regrow; security policy needs to take firm hold and pull at the roots of maritime piracy in Southeast Asia.

Notes

1. Jay L. Batongbacal, "Trends in Anti-Piracy Cooperation in the ASEAN Region", in *Combating "Piracy" and Ship Robbery*, edited by Hamzah Ahmad and Akira Ogawa (Tokyo: Okazaki Institute, 2001), p. 133.
2. "Work Program to Implement the ASEAN Plan of Action to Combat Transnational Crime", 17 May 2002, sec. 3.6–a, b, http://www.aseansec.org/home.htm (accessed 13 January 2005).
3. Batongbacal, "Trends in Anti-Piracy Cooperation", p. 131.
4. Peter Chalk, "Contemporary Maritime Piracy in Southeast Asia", *Studies in Conflict and Terrorism* 21 (March 1997): 96.
5. Adam Young and Mark J. Valencia, "Conflation of Piracy and Terrorism in Southeast Asia: Rectitude and Utility", *Contemporary Southeast Asia* 25, no. 19 (2003): 279.
6. For a good discussion of the potential value of developing coast guards in

the Asia-Pacific region, see Sam Bateman, "Coast Guards: New Forces For Regional Order and Security", *East West Center Asia Pacific Issues*, no. 65 (Honolulu: Sales Office East West Center, January 2003).

7. Samuel Pyeatt Menefee, "Crossing the Line? Maritime Violence, Piracy, Definitions and International Law", in *Combating "Piracy" and Ship Robbery*, edited by Ahmad Ogawa, pp. 68–71. Also, see Comite Maritime International, http://www.comitemaritime.org/singapore/piracy/piracy_ann_a.html (accessed 9 March 2005) for the complete text of the model law.

8. This term is variously defined, but here simply refers to the capacity for local reproduction of economic development, and the ability of local groups to be able to take advantage of development by legitimate means.

9. For a good discussion on issues of corruption in the Indonesian legal system, see Daniel Lev, "The Criminal Regime: Criminal Process in Indonesia", in *Figures of Criminality in Indonesia, the Philippines, and Colonial Vietnam*, edited by Vincente L. Rafael (Ithaca, NY: Southeast Asia Program Publications Southeast Asia Program Cornell University, 1999), pp. 175–92.

10. Menefee, "Crossing the Line?", pp. 65–66.

11. Chalk, "Contemporary Maritime Piracy", pp. 89–90; Jon Vagg, "Rough Seas?", *British Journal of Criminology* 35, no. 1 (1995): 65. Costs may run upwards of $10,000–$25,000 daily, making only the most serious acts of "piracy" worth reporting.

12. Apriadi Gunawan, "Fishermen shun Strait of Malacca for fear pirates", *Jakarta Post*, 10 May 2004, http://www.thejakartapost.com/Archives/ArchivesDet2.asp?FileID=20040510.D02 (accessed 4 February 2005).

13. Only eighteen reported attacks on fishermen worldwide in 2004. "Piracy and Armed Robbery Against Ships Annual Report", 1 January – 31 December 2004, *Piracy Reporting Centre* (Kuala Lumpur: ICC International Maritime Bureau, 2004), p. 13.

14. Young and Valencia, "Conflation of Piracy and Terrorism", p. 271. Associated with the cost benefit analysis of whether to report incidents or not, if members of the crew were seriously injured or killed then these incidents would more likely be reported.

15. John Kerlin, "Navy to shift focus from battles to piracy", *The Australian*, 6 February 2004.

16. For example, see Philippines legal codes detailing punishments for pirates that can include prison sentences up to thirty years or even death sentences ("Crimes Against National Security", Articles 122–123 of the *Revised Penal Code* approved on 8 December 1930 and took effect 1 January 1932, Ramon C. Aquino, "The Revised Penal Code: Act No. 3815", as amended up to Presidential Decree 1877, vol. 1 [Manila, Philippines: Central Lawbook Publishing Co., 1987]; and President Ferdinand E. Marcos, "The Anti-Piracy and Anti-Highway Robbery Law of 1974", Presidential Decree No. 532, *Official Gazette* vol. 70, no. 35 (2 September 1974), 7343.)

17. Menefee, "Crossing the Line?", pp. 66–67.
18. Ian Williams, "Pirates of the Asiatic", *Channel 4 News Singapore*, 19 May 2005 http://www.channel4.com/news/index.html (accessed 4 June 2005).
19. Jason Szep, "After tsunami, fears of a piracy resurgence", Reuters, 25 March 2005, http://reuters.com (accessed 30 March 2005).

Appendix A

Background and Further Details of UNCLOS and SUA

UNCLOS

United Nations Convention on the Law of the Sea (UNCLOS) represents an attempt at codifying a vast array of customary law handed down over the centuries, as well as to create all new bodies of laws, governing and regulating the sea spaces of the world. UNCLOS was put into force after the sixtieth signatory ratified it in 1994. It was negotiated over a period spanning from 1958, when the first articles were drafted, to December 1982, when the Convention was opened for signature in Montego Bay, Jamaica.[1] Approximately 160 countries participated in the negotiations that created UNCLOS, although at present 149 countries have ratified it (or are in the process).[2] From this process has emerged an impressive document trying to tie together various disparate elements of ocean governance. Aside from Article 101 defining piracy, there are several other important aspects of UNCLOS that have impact on the issue of piracy, particularly changes in maritime territorial delineations.

A state has complete sovereign control, as if it was an extension of land, over its "internal waters", whereas in the "territorial seas" states have almost complete sovereign control (including law enforcement), except foreign ships have the "right of transit" (which does not pertain to international straits), and "innocent passage" (which does pertain to international straits, such as the Strait of Malacca).[3] Similarly, in "archipelagic waters" states have almost complete control, but foreign ships have the right to navigate these waters through predetermined "sea lanes" and also through the exercise of "innocent passage".[4] Beyond the 12 mile limit of territorial seas, and outside archipelagic waters, states have the right to claim up to 200 nautical miles from their established baselines as their Exclusive Economic Zone (EEZ), where they enjoy control over economic and environmental development of this area.[5] This presents a problem in Southeast Asia where extending a 200 mile EEZ has created many conflicting territorial claims. These conflicting claims have created zones where legal jurisdiction is unclear, thus making enforcing national laws governing maritime violence difficult to enforce, and international law even more problematic. Furthermore, it is precisely in these areas of conflicting claims, such as the South China Sea, Malacca Strait region, and the Sulu Sea region, where maritime violence is increasingly a problem.

SUA

The inspiration for the Convention for the Suppression of Unlawful Acts Against the Safety of Maritime Navigation (SUA) came indirectly from the 1985 hijacking of the passenger cruise ship *Achille Lauro* in the eastern Mediterranean, at the hands of a few Palestinian Liberation Organization (PLO) operatives.[6] The general ease with which the ship was seized and controlled by so few people, and the international attention the event received prompted the International Maritime Organization (IMO) to address the state of laws regarding political maritime violence in an international setting. In Rome, Italy, in 1988 SUA (which is also called the "Rome Convention" owing to its genesis in Rome) was drafted and opened for signatures, and entered into force 1 March 1992. As of 31 October 2003 there are 95 countries as signatories, covering approximately 76.7 per cent of gross world tonnage shipped by sea, and two years later in 2005 that figure has gone up to 115 contracting states, covering 81 per cent of world tonnage.[7]

Notes

1. Prepared by the Division for Ocean Affairs and the Law of the Sea, Office of Legal Affairs, United Nations, http://www.un.org/Depts/los/convention_agreements/convention_overview_convention.htm.
2. Ibid. Of note, the United States, one of the key negotiators, has not yet ratified UNCLOS.
3. According to UNCLOS territorial seas are defined under Article 3 as: "Every State has the right to establish the breadth of its territorial sea up to a limit not exceeding 12 nautical miles, measured from baselines determined in accordance with this Convention." Internal waters are defined under Article 8 as: "1. Except as provided in Part IV, waters on the landward side of the baseline of the territorial sea form part of the internal waters of the State." Innocent passage is granted within both internal waters and territorial seas, but is extremely limited in scope for internal waters (see Article 8 of

UNCLOS), and is extensively delineated under Articles 18 and 19 of UNCLOS. The "right of transit" is largely delineated in Section 2, Article 37.

4. Archipelagic waters are defined under Article 49 as: "1. The sovereignty of an archipelagic State extends to the waters enclosed by the archipelagic baselines drawn in accordance with article 47, described as archipelagic waters, regardless of their depth or distance from the coast." Ships have the right to travel through archipelagic states via sea lanes, defined by the archipelagic state itself (See Article 53 UNCLOS for further clarification of rights of sea lane passage), and may also exercise "innocent passage" to travel through archipelagic waters (See Article 52 UNCLOS). This right has proven controversial as the United States wants a sea lane through the Java Sea of Indonesia, but Indonesia steadfastly refuses due to the proximity to their national capital of Jakarta to such a sea lane.

5. Under Article 56 of UNCLOS the states' rights in the EEZ is delineated as: "In the exclusive economic zone, the coastal State has: (a) sovereign rights for the purpose of exploring and exploiting, conserving and managing the natural resources, whether living or non-living, of the waters superjacent to the seabed and of the seabed and its subsoil, and with regard to other activities for the economic exploitation and exploration of the zone, such as the production of energy from the water, currents and winds."

6. The *Achille Lauro* incident gained international attention first because of the nature of the hijacking, a large cruise ship full of tourists from around the world, secondly the involvement of a prominent political group, the PLO, and third because during the course of events that unfolded a disabled American was thrown overboard, and killed. This led the United States to test its international authority beyond legal convention, when the hijackers, having negotiated their escape and return to Palestine, were being flown on an Egyptian airliner to that end. To prevent this two U.S. war planes intercepted the airliner and forced it down on Sicily where the hijackers were arrested and then brought into U.S. custody.

7. International Maritime Organization, http://www.imo.org/home.asp.

Appendix B

Piracy Statistics

TABLE 1
Incidents of piracy in Southeast Asia as a percentage of total world incidents

Year	Number of Incidents Recorded in Southeast Asia (SEA)	Number of Incidents Recorded in World	SEA as Percent of World Total Reported (%)
1992	69	106	65
1993	75	103	73
1994	64	90	71
1995	116	188	62
1996	139	2,287	61
1997	113	247	46
1998	96	202	47
1999	164	300	55
2000	259	469	55
2001	173	335	52
2002	165	370	44
2003	188	445	42
2004	171	325	53
Total	1,792	3,408	53

Note: Calculations are based on IMB statistics.

TABLE 2

Incidents of piracy in Indonesia as percentage of incidents reported to the IMB in Southeast Asia, and in the world

Year	Total Incidents Recorded in Indonesia	Indonesia as Percent of SEA (%)	Indonesia as Percent of World (%)
1992	49	71	46
1993	10	13	10
1994	22	34	24
1995	33	28	17
1996	57	41	25
1997	47	42	19
1998	60	62	30
1999	115	70	38
2000	119	46	25
2001	91	53	27
2002	103	55	28
2003	121	64	27
2004	93	54	27
Total	920	51	27

Note: Calculations based on IMB Statistics.

Bibliography

BOOKS AND ARTICLES

Abbot, Jason and Neil Renwick. "Pirates? Maritime Piracy and Societal Security in Southeast Asia". *Pacifica Review* 11, no. 1 (February 1999): 7–24.

ABC Radio Australia. "Indonesia says illegal fishing crackdown is successful". http://www.eurocbc.org/indonesian_sinking_policy_curbs_illegal_fishing_02jan2004page1390.html (accessed 3 February 2005).

Abhyankar, Jayant. "Piracy and Ship Robbery: A Growing Menace". In *Combating Piracy and Ship Robbery: Charting the Future in Asia Pacific Waters*, edited by Hamzah Ahmad and Akira Ogawa, pp. 10–61. Tokyo: Okazaki Institute, 2001.

Abidin, Andi Zainal. *Sekali Lagi La Ma'dukelleng Arung Singkang* [Once Again La Ma'dukelleng Arung Singkang]. Ujung Pandang: Panitia Dasa Warsa IKIP, 1975.

Acharya, Amitav. "Transnational Production and Security: Southeast Asia's 'Growth Triangles'". *Contemporary Southeast Asia* 17, no. 2 (September 1995): 173–85.

Ahmad, Hamzah B. "Piracy and Ship Robbery: An Introduction". In *Combating Piracy and Ship Robbery: Charting the Future in Asia Pacific Waters*, edited by Hamzah Ahmad and Akira Ogawa, pp. 1–9. Tokyo: Okazaki Institute, 2001.

Ahmad, Raja Ali Haji ibn. *The Precious Gift: Tuhfat al-Nafis*, translated by Virginia Matheson and Barbara Watson-Andaya. Kuala Lumpur: Oxford University Press, 1982.

Alagappa, Muthiah. "Introduction". In *Political Legitimacy in Southeast Asia*, edited by Muthiah Alagappa. Stanford: Stanford University Press, 1995.

Andaya, Barbara Watson. "The Role of the Anak Raja". *Journal of Southeast Asian Studies* 7, no. 2 (1976): 162–86.

——. "Recreating a Vision". *Bijdragen tot de Taal-, Land- en Volkekunde* 153, no. 4 (1997): 483–507.

—— and Leonard Y. Andaya. *A History of Malaysia*. 2nd ed. Honolulu: University of Hawaii Press, 2001.

Andaya, Leonard. *The Kingdom of Johor, 1641–1728*. Kuala Lumpur: Oxford University Press, 1975.

——. "Interactions with the Outside World and Adaptation in Southeast Asian Society, 1500–1800". In *The Cambridge History of Southeast Asia*, vol. 1, Part 2, edited by Nicholas Tarling. Cambridge: Cambridge University Press, 1999.

Anderson, J. L. "Piracy and World History: An Economic Perspective on Maritime Predation". *Journal of World History* 6, no. 2 (1995): 175–99.

Asia Pulse. "Indonesia's Losses from Foreign Fish Poachers Down 50 Pct", 24 September 2003, Sec. Northern Territory Regional.

Asian Wall Street Journal. "Malaysia, Thailand to Start Border Patrols", 12 January 2004.

Associated Press. "Report: Chinese May be Sanctioning Piracy", 9 March 1994.

Augustine, Saint Bishop of Hippo. *The City of God Against the Pagans*, translated and edited by R. W. Dyson. Cambridge: Cambridge University Press, 1998.

Aung-Thwin, Michael. "Spirals in Early Southeast Asian and Burmese History". *Journal of Interdisciplinary History* XXI, no. 4 (Spring 1991): 575–602.

———. "Parochial Universalism, Democracy *Jihad*, and the Orientalist Image of Burma". *Pacific Affairs* 76, no. 4 (Winter 2001–02): 483–505.

Australian, The. "Piracy Resurgence on the High Seas", 8 November 1978, p. 11.

Bankoff, Greg. *Crime, Society, and the State in the Nineteenth Century Philippines*. Manila: Ateneo de Manila University Press, 1996.

Barnard, Timothy. "Multiple Centers of Authority". Ph.D. dissertation, University of Hawaii at Manoa, 1998.

Bateman, Sam. "Maritime Transnational Violence: Problems of Control and Jurisdiction". Paper presented at the Seminar on "Transnational Crime" at the APCSS Biennial Conference in Honolulu, 16–18 July 2002.

———. "Coast Guards: New Forces For Regional Order and Security". East West Center Asia Pacific Issues, no. 65. Honolulu: Sales Office East West Center, January 2003.

Batongbacal, Jay L. "Trends in Anti-Piracy Cooperation in the ASEAN Region". In *Combating "Piracy" and Ship Robbery*, edited by Hamzah Ahmad and Akira Ogawa, pp. 104–33. Tokyo: Okazaki Institute, 2001.

Bedi, Bishen. "New Deal". *Malaysian Business*, 1 January 2002, Sec. Region, p. 64.

Bednarik, Robert G. "An Experiment in Pleistocene Seafaring". *International Journal of Nautical Archaeology* 27, no. 2 (1998): 139–49.

Bello, Walden. "The Insecurity of Asia's Financial Crisis". *Peace Review* 11, no. 3 (September 1999): 393–99. *Academic Search Premier* online database.

Bellwood, Peter. *Prehistory of the Indo-Malayan Archipelago*. Rev. ed. Honolulu: University of Hawaii Press, 1997.

Bingley, Barret. "U.S. interests in Malacca Straits". *Jakarta Post*, 17 July 2004. http://www.thejakartapost.com/Archives/ArchivesDet2.asp?FileID = 20040707.E03 (accessed 14 January 2005).

Boutwell, Jeffery and Micheal Klare. "Small Arms and Light Weapons: Controlling the Real Instruments of War". *Arms Control Today* 28 (August/September 1998): 15–23.

Bradsher, Keith. "Warnings From Al Qaeda Stir Fear That Terrorists May Attack Oil Tankers". *New York Times*, 12 December 2002, Sec. A.

——. "Attacks on Chemical Ships in Southeast Asia Seem to be Piracy, Not Terrorism". *New York Times*, 27 March 2003, Sec. A.

Buhler, Philip A. "New Struggle with an Old Menace: Towards a Revised Definition of Maritime 'Piracy'". *Currents: International Trade Law Journal* (Winter 1999). LexisLaw electronic printout 17pp.

Burnett, John. *Dangerous Waters: Modern Piracy and Terror on the High Seas*. New York: Dutton, 2002.

Businessworld. "Chinese Military, Moro Insurgents Commit Piracy in South China Sea", 13 May 1999. *ProQuest* online database.

Campo, Joseph N. F. M. "Discourse without Discussion: Representations of Piracy in Colonial Indonesia 1816–25". *Journal of Southeast Asian Studies* 34, no. 2 (June 2003): 199–216.

Carpenter, William M. and David G. Wiencek. "Maritime Piracy in Asia". In *Asian Security Handbook*, edited by William M. Carpenter and David G. Wiencek, pp. 88–98. New York: Armonk, 2000.

Cash, Johnny. *Busted*. Columbia Country Records compact disk C3K 65557, CK 65559, DIDP 095201.

Chaikin, Greg. "Maritime Regimes and Piracy in East Asia: Can Japan Climb Aboard?". Paper presented at the conference "People and the Sea II: Conflicts, Threats and Opportunities", Amsterdam, 1 August 2003.

Chalk, Peter. "Contemporary Maritime Piracy in Southeast Asia". *Studies in Conflict and Terrorism* 21 (March 1997): 87–112.

——. *Low Intensity Conflict in Southeast Asia*. Conflict Studies, no. 305/306. Warwickshire, England: Research Institute for the Study of Conflict and Terrorism, 1998.

——. *Non-Military Security and Global Order*. London: Macmillan Press, 2000.

Chou, Cynthia. "Contesting the Tenure of Territoriality". *Bijdragen tot de Taal-, Land- en Volkenkunde* 153 no. 4 (1997): 605–29.

Christie, Jan Wisseman. "State Formation in Early Maritime Southeast Asia: A Consideration of the Theories and the Data". *Bijdragen tot de Taal-, Land- en Volkenkunde* 151, no. 2 (1995): 235–88.

Cottrill, Ken. "Modern Marauders". *Popular Mechanics* 174, no. 12 (December 1997): 78–80.

Course, Captain A. G. *Pirates of the Eastern Seas*. London: Cox and Lyman Limited, 1966.

Crouch, Harold. *The Army and Politics in Indonesia*. Ithaca: Cornell University Press, 1978.

Defoe, Daniel. *A General History of the Robberies and Murders of the Most Notorious Pyrates*. New York: Garland Publishing, 1972.

Dery, Luis C. "Moro Raids and Their Impact on Luzon and the Visayas: The Non-Spanish and Non-Muslim View". Paper presented at the 34th International Congress for Asian and Northern African Studies (ICANAS), University of Hong Kong, 1993.

Deutsche Presse-Agentur. "Pirates of the Malacca Straits on a roll", 28 September 2003, Sec. Miscellaneous.

———. "Malaysia launches massive operation to crack down on sea smuggling", 24 October 2004, Sec. Miscellaneous.

Dillion, Paul. "Did tsunamis ruin pirates of Sumatra?". *The Globe and Mail*, 25 January 2005. http://www.theglobeandmail.com/ (accessed 26 January 2005).

Dinakar, Sethuraman. "The Jolly Roger Flies High ... As Piracy Feeds the Hungry". *Business Week International Editions*, vol. 3630, 24 May 1999, Sec. Spotlight on the Strait of Malacca, p. 4.

Djalal, Dino Patti. *The Geopolitics of Indonesia's Maritime Territorial Policy*. Jakarta: Centre for Strategic and International Studies, 1996.

Dunn, F. L. and D. F. Dunn. "Maritime Adaptations and Exploitation of Marine Resources in Sundaic Southeast Asian Prehistory". In *Prehistoric Indonesia*, edited by Pieter van de Velde, pp. 244–71. Foris Publications, 1984.

Dupont, Alan. *East Asia Imperiled: Transnational Challenges to Security*. Cambridge: Cambridge University Press, 2001.

Economist. "Those in Peril on the Sea", vol. 344, no. 8029 (9 August 1997): 40. *ProQuest* online database.

———. "South Sea Piracy", 18 December 1999, U.S. ed.

———. "War Without End", vol. 367, no. 8322 (3 May 2003): 46.

———. "How Not to Deter Refugees; By Allowing Them to be Killed by Pirates". U.S. ed., Sec. World Politics and Current Affairs, p. 16. *LexisNexis Academic* online database.

Engelhardt, Richard A. and Pamela Rumball Rogers. "The Phuket Project Revisited: The Ethno-archaeology Through Time of Maritime Adapted Communities in Southeast Asia". *Journal of the Siam Society* 85, (1997): 17–33.

Fabey, Michael. "Pirates Private and Public". *Traffic World* 256, no. 10, p. 26. *ProQuest* online database.

Farnham, Alan. "Pirates". *Fortune*, 15 July 1991.

Fegan, Brian. "Plundering the Sea". *Inside Indonesia* (January–March 2003). http://www.insideindonesia.org/edit73/Fegan%20fishing.htm (accessed 2 February 2005).

Flynn, Matthew. "China Promises Crackdown as it Strives to Escape Image of a Safe Haven for Pirates". *Lloyd's List International*, 24 February 1999.

Freudmann, Aviva. "Scotland Yard Links Increase in Piracy to Organized Crime". *Journal of Commerce*, 1 February 1999, Sec. Maritime, p. 2B.

Garmon, Tina. "International Law of the Sea: Reconciling the Law of 'Piracy' and Terrorism in the Wake of September 11th". *The Maritime Lawyer*, 27 March 2002.

Gibson-Hill, C. A. "The Orang Laut of the Singapore River and the Sampan Panjang". *Royal Asiatic Society Journal Malayan Branch* XXV, Pt. 1 (1952): 161–74.

Gomes, Edwin H. *Seventeen Years Among the Sea Dyaks of Borneo*. Philadelphia: J. B. Lippincott Company, 1911.

Goodman, Timothy H. "Leaving the Corsairs Name to Other Times: How to Enforce the Law of Sea 'Piracy' in the 21st Century Through Regional International Agreements". *Case Western Reserve Journal of International Law* (Winter 1999). LexisLaw.

Gosse, Philip. *The History of Piracy*. New York: Tudor Publishing Company, 1934.

Green, Leslie. *The Authority of the State*. Oxford: Clarendon Press, 1988.

Gunawan, Apriadi. "Fishermen shun Strait of Malacca for fear of pirates". *Jakarta Post*, 10 May 2004. http://www.thejakartapost.com/Archives/ArchivesDet2.asp?FileID = 20040510.D02 (accessed 4 February 2005).

Hagan, Kenneth J. *This People's Navy*. New York: The Free Press, 1991.

Hall, D. G. E. *A History of Southeast Asia*. New York: St Martin's Press, 1968.

Hall, Kenneth R. *Maritime Trade and State Development in Early Southeast Asia*. Honolulu: University of Hawaii Press, 1985.

Headrick, Daniel R. *The Tools of Empire*. New York: Oxford University Press, 1981.

Hobsbawm, Eric. *Bandits*. New York: Pantheon Books, 1981.

Hoshour, Cathy A. "Resettlement and the Politicization of Ethnicity in Indonesia". *Bijdragen tot de Taal-, Land- en Volkekunde* 153, no. 4 (1997): 557–76.

Jakarta Post. "Navy to buy two submarines". 19 September 2003, Sec. Front page.

Japan Economic Newswire. "Japan to Send Patrol Vessel to Singapore for Anti-Piracy", 19 November 2003, Sec. International News.

Jenkins, David. "The Military's Secret Cache". *Far Eastern Economic Review* 107, no. 6 (8 February 1980): 70–74.

Jinks, Beth. "Step up Security Measures, Harbour Craft Warned". *Shipping Times*, 14 January 2004, Sec. News

Johnstone, Ralph. "The Sea Gypsies". *Asia Week*, 21 April 1993, pp. 46–55.

Junker, L. "Craft Good Specialization and Prestige Goods Exchange in Philippine Chiefdoms of the Fifteenth and Sixteenth Centuries". *Asian Perspectives* 32, no. 1 (1999): 1–36.

Kahin, Audrey. *Regional Dynamics of the Indonesian Revolution*. Honolulu: University of Hawaii Press, 1985.

Karakker, Cyrus H. *Piracy was a Business*. Rindge, New Hampshire: R.R. Smith, 1953.

Kawamura, Sumihiko. "Regional Cooperation Against Piracy and Armed Robbery". In *Combating Piracy and Ship Robbery: Charting the Future in Asia Pacific Waters*, edited by Hamzah Ahmad and Akira Ogawa, pp. 138–59. Okazaki Institute: Tokyo, 2001.

Keppel, Henry and James Brooke. *The Expedition of the H.M.S. Dido*. New York: Oxford University Press, 1991.

Kerlin, John. "Navy to shift focus from battles to piracy". *The Australian*, 6 February 2004.

Keyuan, Zou. "Enforcing the Law of Piracy in the South China Sea". *Journal of Maritime Law & Commerce* (January 2000): 107–17. LexisNexis Academic online database.

――. "Quelling Sea Piracy in East Asia". Paper presented at the conference "People and the Sea II: Conflicts, Threats and Opportunities", Amsterdam, 1 August 2003.

Kingsbury, Damien. *Power Politics and the Indonesian Military*. London: Routledge Curzon, 2003.

Kompas. "TNI AL Siap Hadapi Pembajakan di Laut" [Indonesian Navy is Ready to Face Piracy at Sea], 29 June 2001. http://www.kompas.com/kompas-cetak/0106/29/jatim/tnia46.htm (accessed 27 March 2004).

――. "Sindikat Bajak Laut Internasional Kemungkinan Beraksi Di Indonesia", 18 September 2003. http://www.kompas.com (accessed 12 January 2005).

――. "Selat Sunda Rawan Perompakan" [Southern Sunda Disturbed by Piracy], 9 October 2003, Sec. Nusantara online. http://www.kompas.com/kompas-cetak/0310/09/daerah/613872.htm (accessed 27 March 2004).

――. "Polisi Tangkap Kawanan Perompak Nelayan di Laut" [Police Arrest Fisherman Pirate's Accomplice at Sea], 15 June 2004. http://www.kompas.com (accessed 20 January 2005).

――. "TNI AL Tangkap Otak Perompakan Dua Kapal Asing di Natuna" [Indonesian Navy Arrests Mastermind of Two Pirated Foreign Ships in Natuna], 8 August 2004. http://www.kompas.com (accessed 13 January 2005).

――. "Selat Bangka Masih Rawan Perompakan" [Southern Bangka Still Troubled by Piracy], 17 November 2004. http://www.kompas.com (accessed 13 January 2005).

――. "Takut Perompak, Nelayan Tak Melaut" [Afraid of Piracy Fishermen Don't Go to Sea], 14 December 2004. http://www.kompas.com (accessed 13 Janaury 2005).

Legge, James. *A Record of Buddhistic Kingdoms*. Oxford: Clarendon Press, 1886. Unaltered Reprint, New York: Paragon Book Reprint Corp., Dover Publications, Inc., 1965.

Leifer, Micheal. *Dilemmas of Statehood in Southeast Asia*. Vancouver: University of British Columbia Press, 1972.

Lenhart, Lioba. "Ethnic Minority Policy and National Development in Indonesia". In *Nationalism and Ethnicity in Southeast Asia*, edited by Ingrid Wessel, pp. 577–604. Munster, Germany: Lit Verlag, 1993.

Leur, J. C. van. *Indonesian Trade and Society: Essays in Asian Social and Economic History*. Bandung: Sumur Bandung, 1960.

Lev, Daniel. "The Criminal Regime: Criminal Process in Indonesia". In *Figures of Criminality in Indonesia, the Philippines, and Colonial Vietnam*, edited by Vincente L. Rafael, pp. 175–92. Ithaca, NY: Southeast Asia Program Publications Southeast Asia Program Cornell University, 1999.

Lewis, Dianne. *Jan Compagnie in the Straits of Malacca, 1641–1795*. Athens, Ohio: Ohio University Center for International Studies, 1995.

Lintner, Bertil. "Crime — and Punishment?". *Far Eastern Economic Review* 165, no. 29 (25 July 2002): 46–50. *ProQuest* online database.

Liss, Carolin. "Maritime Piracy in Southeast Asia". *Southeast Asian Affairs 2003*, pp. 52–68. Singapore: Institute of Southeast Asian Studies, 2003.

Manguin, P. Y. "City-States and City-State Culture in pre-15th Century Southeast Asia". In *A Comparative Study of Thirty City-State Cultures*, edited by M. H. Hansen, pp. 409–16. Historisk-filosofiske Skrifter 21. Copenhagen: The Royal Danish Academy of Sciences and Letters.

May, Ronald J. "Muslim Mindanao: Four Years After the Peace". *Southeast Asian Affairs 2001*, pp. 263–78. Singapore: Institute of Southeast Asian Studies, 2001. *Academic Search Premier* online database.

McGeown, Kate. "Aceh Rebels Blamed for Piracy". BBC News, 8 September 2003. http://news.bbc.co.uk/1/hi/world/asia-pacific/3090136.stm (accessed 14 March 2005).

Menefee, Samuel Pyeatt. "Crossing the Line? Maritime Violence, Piracy, Definitions and International Law". In *Combating Piracy and Ship Robbery: Charting the Future in Asia Pacific Waters*, edited by Hamzah Ahmad and Akira Ogawa, pp. 60–88. Tokyo: Okazaki Institute, 2001.

Mo, John. "Options to Combat Maritime Piracy in Southeast Asia". *Ocean Development & International Law* 33, no. 3-4 (2002): 343–58.

Mubyarto. "Riau Progress and Poverty", translated by Robson, Chou, and Derks. *Bijdragen tot de Taal-, Land- en Volkekunde* 153, no. 4 (1997): 542–56.

Mukundun, P. "Piracy and Armed Robbery against Ships Today". Paper presented at the conference "People and the Sea II: Conflicts, Threats and Opportunities", Amsterdam, 1 August 2003.

Murray, Dian. *Pirates of the South China Coast 1790–1810*. Stanford: Stanford University Press, 1987.

"National Survey of Corruption in Indonesia, A Final Report December 2001". Partnership for Governance Reform in Indonesia, Jakarta, 2001.

Nincic, Donna J. "Sea Lane Security and U.S. Maritime Trade: Choke Points as Scarce Resources". In *Globalization and Maritime Power*, edited by Sam J. Tangredi. Washington, D.C.: National Defense University Press, 2002.

Nordholt, H.S. "The Jago in the Shadow: Crime and 'Order' in the Colonial State in Java". *Review of Indonesian and Malaysian Affairs* 25, no. 1 (1991): 74–91.

Ong, G. Gerard. "Ships Can Be Dangerous Too". Paper presented at the conference "People and the Sea II: Conflicts, Threats and Opportunities", Amsterdam, 1 August 2003.

Osler, David. "Global Piracy Bill". *Lloyd's List International*, 11 December 2002, p. 1.

Osman, Salim. "Indonesian military seeks $10b budget". *Straits Times Interactive*, 26 February 2005. http://straitstimes.asia1.com.sg (accessed 26 February 2005).

Paik, Jin-Hyun, and Anthony Bergin. "Maritime Security in the Asia Pacific". In *Asia's Emerging Regional Order*, edited by William T. Tow, Ramesh Chandra Thakur, and In-Taek Hyun, pp. 177–91. Tokyo and New York: United Nations University Press, 2000.

Passas, Nikos. "Globalization and Transnational Crime: Effects of Criminogenic Asymmetries". In *Combating Transnational Crime*, edited by P. Williams and D. Vlassis, pp. 22–56. London/Portland, OR: Frank Cass, 2001.

Patinio, Ferdinand. "CBCP Official Says Commission to Probe Sasa Wharf Bombing". *Manila Times*, 18 August 2003, Sec. Top Stories. http://www.manilatimes.net/national/2003/aug/18/top_stories/20030818top9.html (accessed 27 March 2004).

Perotin-Dumon, Anne. "The Pirate and the Emperor". In *The Political Economy of Merchant Empires*, edited by James D. Tracy, pp. 196–227. Cambridge: Cambridge University Press, 1991.

Peterson, M. J. "An Historical Perspective on the Incidents of Piracy". In *Piracy at Sea*, edited by Eric Ellen, pp. 41–60. Paris: International Chamber of Commerce, International Maritime Bureau, 1989.

Piracy and Armed Robbery Against Ships Annual Report, 1 January – 31 December 2003. Piracy Reporting Centre. Kuala Lumpur: ICC International Maritime Bureau, 2003.

Piracy and Armed Robbery Against Ships Annual Report, 1 January – 31 December 2004. Piracy Reporting Centre. Kuala Lumpur: ICC International Maritime Bureau, 2004.

Pringle, Robert. *Rajahs and Rebels: The Ibans of Sarawak under Brooke Rule, 1841–1941*. Ithaca: Cornell University Press, 1970.

Reme, Ahmad. "Pirates and terrorists not natural allies". *Straits Times*, 29 June 2004. http://straitstimes.com (accessed 29 June 2004).

Republika. "DKP Bertekad Terus Berantas Pencurian Ikan" [Ministry of Maritime Affairs and Fisheries Fight Illegal Fishing], 31 January 2005. http://www.republika.co.id/koran_detail.asp?id=185768&kat_id=4 (accessed 2 February 2005).

Reuters. "Tsunami may have washed away pirate problem", 10 February 2005. http://www.stuff.co.nz/stuff/ (accessed 25 February 2005).

———. "Singapore navy to escort commercial ships", 28 February 2005. http://www.arabtimesonline.com/arabtimes/breaking news (accessed 1 March 2005).

Rigg, Jonathan. *Southeast Asia: The Human Landscape of Modernization and Development*. 2nd ed. London: Routledge, 2003.

Rubin, Alfred P. *The Law of "Piracy"*. 2nd ed. New York: Transnational Publishers, Inc., 1998.

Said, Edward. *Orientalism*. New York: Vintage Books, 1978.

Sandin, Benedict. *The Sea Dayaks of Borneo*. Lansing: Michigan State University Press, 1967.

Sather, C. "Sea Nomads and Rainforest Hunter-Gatherers: Foraging Adaptations in the Indo-Malaysian Archipelago". In *The Austronesians: Historical and Comparative Perspectives*, edited by P. Bellwood, J. J. Fo, and D. Tryon, pp. 229–68. Canberra: Department of Anthropology, Research School of Pacific and Asian Studies, Australian National University, 1995.

———. *The Bajau Laut*. Kuala Lumpur: Oxford University Press, 1997.

Scott, William Henry. *Barangay*. Manila: Ateneo De Manila University Press, 1999.

SCTV 6. "Nelayan Belawan Takut Melaut" [Fishermen from Belawan are Afraid to go to Sea], 26 June 2003, sec. Laporan Daerah, http://www.liputan6.com/fullnews/59141.html (accessed 27 February 2004).

Shulze, Kirsten E. "The Struggle for an Independent Aceh". *Studies in Conflict and Terrorism* 26, no. 4 (2003): 241–72.

Siboro, Tiarma. "More Countries to Patrol Malacca Strait". *Jakarta Post*, 7 August 2004. http://www.thejakartapost.com/Archives/ArchivesDet2.asp?FileID = 20040807.B01 (accessed 4 February 2005).

Simhan, Raja T. E. "Wave of Piracy Hits Asia-Pacific Waters". *Businessline* (Islamabad), 17 November 2003. *ProQuest* online database.

Siregar, Irwan and Syamsul Anam et al. "Aman Berkat Praktik Ali Baba" [It is Peaceful because of the Practice of Ali Baba]. *Gamma* 2, no. 5, pp. 74–75.

Soesastro, Hadi. "Globalization, Development, and Security in Southeast Asia: An Overview". In *Development and Security in Southeast Asia*, edited by David B. Dewitt and Carolina G. Hernandez, vol. 3, *Globalization*, pp. 19–40. Hants, England: Ashgate Publishing Company, 2003.

Straits Times. "S'pore accedes to anti-maritime terror pact", 4 February 2004, Sec. Singapore.

Stuart, Robert. *In Search of Pirates: A Modern-Day Odyssey*. Edinburgh: Mainstream, 2002.

Sukma, Rizal. "The Security Problematique of Globalization and Development: The Case of Indonesia". In *Development and Security in Southeast Asia*, edited by David B. Dewitt and Carolina G. Hernandez, vol. 3, *Globalization*, pp. 233–58. Hants, England: Ashgate Publishing Company, 2003.

Sulaiman, Dr. M. Isa. *Aceh Merdeka: Ideologi, Kepemimpinan dan Gerakan* [Free Aceh: Ideology, Leadership, and Political Movement]. Jakarta: Pustaka Al-Kaustar, 2000.

Szep, Jason. "After tsunami, tears of a piracy resurgence". Reuters, 25 March 2005. http://reuters.com (accessed 30 March 2005).

Tagliacozzo, Eric. *Secret Trades of the Straits: Smuggling and State-formation along a Southeast Asian Frontier, 1870–1910*. Hartford: Yale University Press, 1999.

———. "Kettle on a Slow Boil: Batavia's Threat Perceptions in the Indies Outer Islands, 1870–1910". *Journal of Southeast Asian Studies* 31, no. 1 (March 2000): 70–100.

Tarling, Nicholas. *Piracy and Politics in the Malay World*. Melbourne: F.W. Cheshire, 1963.

———. *Southeast Asia: A Modern History*. Victoria: Oxford University Press, 2001.

Teitler, Ger. "Piracy in Southeast Asia: A Historical Comparison". *MAST* 1, no. 1 (2002): 67–83. http://www.marecentre.nl/mast/mastmastnewvol1.1.html (accessed 27 March 2004).

Teo, Karen. "New Piracy Attacks Put Spotlight on Indonesia". *Energy Intelligence Group, Inc.*, 18 August 2003, Sec. Feature Stories.

Thomson, Janice E. *Mercenaries, Pirates, and Sovereigns*. Princeton: Princeton University Press, 1994.

Torode, Greg. "Probe into Stolen Ship Racket Leads to HK Firm". *South China Morning Post*, 25 July 1994, p. 4.

Trocki, Carl A. *Prince of Pirates*. Singapore: Singapore University Press, 1979.

Urquhart, Donald. "Malacca Strait users urged to help pay for safety aids". *Business Times* (Singapore), 14 October 2003, Sec. Shipping Times.

———. "Pirate Attacks Will Lead to Disaster in Malacca Straits". *Shipping Times*, 29 October 2003, Sec. News.

Vagg, Jon. "Rough Seas?". *British Journal of Criminology* 35, no. 1 (1995): 63–79.

Vaknin, Sam. "Treasure Island Revisited". *Financial News*, 19 July 2002, p. 2. LexisNexis Academic online database.

Valencia, Mark J. "Troubled Waters". *Harvard International Review* 16, no. 2 (Spring 1994): 12. *Academic Search Premier* online database.

———. "Regional Maritime Regime Building: Prospects in Northeast and Southeast Asia". *Ocean Development & International Law* 31, no. 3 (Jul–Sep 2000): 223. *Academic Search Premier* online database.

Vieira, Monica Brito. "Mare Liberum vs. Mare Clausum". *Journal of the History of Ideas* 64, no. 3 (July 2003): 361–77.

Wagner, Ulla. *Colonialism and Iban Warfare*. Stockholm: OBE-Tryck, 1972.

Warren, James Francis. "Slave Markets and Exchange in the Malay World". *Journal of Southeast Asian Studies* 8, no. 2 (1977): 162–75.

———. "Who Were the Balangingi Samal?". *Journal of Asian Studies* 37, no. 3 (1978): 477–90.

———. *The Sulu Zone*. Singapore: Singapore University Press, 1981.

———. *The Global Economy and the Sulu Zone*. Quezon City: New Day Publishers, 2000.

———. *Iranun and Balangingi: Globalization, Maritime Raiding and the Birth of Ethnicity*. Quezon City: New Day Publishers, 2002.

———. "A Tale of Two Centuries". ARI Working Thesis, no. 2, June 2003. http://www.ari.nus.edu.sg/pub/wps2003.htm (accessed 27 March 2004).

Weeks, Stanley. "Piracy and Regional Security". In *Combating Piracy and Ship Robbery: Charting the Future in Asia Pacific Waters*, edited by Hamzah Ahmad and Akira Ogawa, pp. 89–103. Tokyo: Okazaki Institute, 2001.

Westlake, Michael. "But Is It Safe? Sea and Air Accidents, Piracy Plague Cargo".

Far Eastern Economic Review 155, no. 46 (19 November 1992): 45. *ProQuest* online database.

Wheatley, Paul. *The Golden Khersonese*. Kuala Lumpur: University of Malaya Press, 1961.

Whitehead, C. Esq. *Lives and Exploits of English Highwaymen, Pirates and Robbers*. London: Charles Daly, 1839.

Williams, Ian. "Pirates of the Asiatic". *Channel 4 News Singapore*, 19 May 2005. http://www.channel4.com/news/index.html (accessed 4 June 2005).

Wolters, O. W. *Early Indonesian Commerce*. Ithaca: Cornell University Press, 1967.

———. *The Fall of Srivijaya*. Ithaca: Cornell University Press, 1970.

———. *History, Culture, and Region in Southeast Asian Perspectives*. Southeast Asia Program Publications, no. 26 revised. Ithaca: Cornell Southeast Asia Programs Publications, 1999.

Xinhua News Agency. "Indonesia, Malaysia to Enhance Cooperation to Curb Smuggling", 28 August 2003.

Yonhap. "Global Shipping Industry Expects another Boom Year". *Asia Pulse*, 7 January 2004, Sec. Northern Territory Regional.

Young, Adam and Mark J. Valencia. "Conflation of Piracy and Terrorism in Southeast Asia: Rectitude and Utility". *Contemporary Southeast Asia* 25, no. 19 (2003): 269–83.

Yulianti, T. "Bajak Laut" [Sea Pirates]. *Suara Pembaruan Daily*, 13 June 2003. http://mail2.factsoft.de/pipermail/national/2002-June/005671.html (accessed 27 March 2004).

WEBSITES

ASEAN Secretariat. http://www.aseansec.org/home.htm (accessed 16 March 2005).

Australian Maritime Safety Authority. http://imo.amsa.gov.au/public/parties/sua88.html (accessed 4 June 2005).

Badan Pusat Statistik, Republik Indonesia. http://www.bps.go.id/index.shtml (accessed 28 March 2004).

Comite Maritime International. http://www.comitemaritime.org/singapore/piracy/piracy_ann_a.html (accessed 9 March 2005).

Country Analysis Briefs. http://www.eia.doe.gov/emeu/cabs/choke.html (cited 9 March 2005).

Division for Ocean Affairs and the Law of the Sea, Office of Legal Affairs, United Nations, http://www.un.org/Depts/los/convention_agreements/convention_overview_convention.htm (accessed 25 January 2005).

Food and Agriculture Organization of the United Nations. http://www.fao.org/fi/fcp/fcp.asp (accessed 28 March 2004).

International Crime Services, International Maritime Bureau. http://www.iccwbo.org/ccs/menu_imb_bureau.asp (accessed 27 March 2004).

International Maritime Bureau-Piracy Reporting Centre. http://www.iccwbo.org/ccs/menu_imb_piracy.asp (accessed 27 March 2004).

International Maritime Bureau-Piracy Reporting Centre. Available at: http://www.icc-ccs.org/prc/overview.php (accessed 26 January 2005).

International Maritime Organization. http://www.imo.org/home.asp (accessed 27 March 2004).

Interpol, International Crime Statistics. http://www.interpol.int/Public/Statistics/ICS/downloadList.asp (accessed 27 March 2004).

Llyods Registry. http://www.lr.org/market_sector/marine/maritime-security/faqs.htm (accessed 27 March 2004).

Maritime History and Naval Heritage. http://www.cronab.demon.co.uk/gen1.htm (accessed 27 March 2004).

Nationmaster.com. http://www.nationmaster.com/encyclopedia/Frigate (accessed 27 March 2004).

Philippines National Statistics Office. http://www.census.gov.ph/ (accessed 28 March 2004).

World Trade Organization. http://www.wto.org/english/thewto_e/minist_e/min96_e/maritime.htm (accessed 27 March 2004).

———. News Press Release, Press/386, 25 October 2004. http://www.wto.org/english/news_e/pres04_e/pr386_e.htm (accessed 21 February 2005).

GOVERNMENT DOCUMENTS AND TREATIES

Convention for the Suppression of Unlawful Acts Against the Safety of Maritime Navigation Rome: March 10, 1988. http://edoc.mpil.de/conference-on-terrorism/related/uc.cfm. (accessed 27 March 2004).

"Crimes Against National Security". Articles 122–123 of the Revised Penal Code approved on 8 December 1930 and took effect 1 January 1932, Ramon C. Aquino. "The Revised Penal Code: Act No. 3815", as amended up to Presidential Decree 1877, vol. 1 (Manila: Central Lawbook Publishing Co., 1987).

Joint Communiqué the First ASEAN Plus Three Ministerial Meeting on Transnational Crime (AMMTC + 3) Bangkok, January 2004. http://www.aseansec.org/home.htm (accessed 13 January 2005).

Joint Communiqué of the Second ASEAN Ministerial Meeting on Transnational Crime, January 2004. http://www.aseansec.org/home.htm (accessed 13 January 2005).

Manila Declaration on the Prevention and Control of Transnational Crime, February 1998. http://www.aseansec.org/home.htm (accessed 13 January 2005).

Memorandum of Understanding Between the Governments of the Member Countries of the Association of Southeast Asian Nations (ASEAN) and the Government of the People's Republic of China on Cooperation in the Field of Non-traditional Security Issues, November 2002. http://www.aseansec.org/home.htm (accessed 13 January 2005).

President Ferdinand E. Marcos. "The Anti-Piracy and Anti-Highway Robbery Law of 1974". Presidential Decree No. 532, Official Gazette vol. 70, no. 35 (2 September 1974): 7343.

United Nations Convention of the Law of the Sea Montego Bay, Jamaica, 10 December 1982 http://www.un.org/Depts/los/convention_agreements/texts/unclos/closindx.htm (accessed 27 March 2004).

Work Program to Implement the ASEAN Plan of Action to Combat Transnational Crime, 17 May 2002. http://www.aseansec.org/home.htm (accessed 13 January 2005).

Index

ABOUT THE AUTHOR

Adam J. Young was born and raised in Northeastern Vermont, and attended the University of Vermont (UVM) in Burlington, where he received Bachelors Degree in History and Geology with honours. While at UVM Adam studied abroad in Indonesia where he first developed his interest in Southeast Asian affairs, particularly dealing with Indonesia. In the years following UVM Adam studied Indonesian, successfully completing two intensive immersion courses in Indonesian.

He attended the University of Hawaii at Manoa in Honolulu, Hawaii where he received his Masters Degree in Asian Studies, with a focus on Southeast Asia in 2004. Adam also had the honour of being affiliated with the East-West Center where he had the opportunity to work with talented researchers such as Mark Valencia, whom Adam co-published two articles with, and to live with a community from all over the Asia-Pacific region dedicated to mutual understanding as well as outstanding research. Adam's graduate work focused on maritime security and the issue of piracy in Southeast Asia, but also heavily involved history, culture, and language.

Currently his interests have shifted focus from specific security policy issues such as piracy to a more general approach to security, emphasizing conflict transformation, understanding conflict as an intrinsic part of life from which we can learn about each other and ourselves. Adam is currently working for a non-profit mediation organization on the North Shore.